Banding Together for a Cause

Banding Together for a Cause

Proven Strategies for Revenue and Awareness Generation

Rachel Armbruster

WILEY

John Wiley & Sons, Inc.

Published by John Wiley & Sons, Inc., Hoboken, New Jersey.
Published simultaneously in Canada.

No rights in the LIVESTRONG mark are granted and LIVESTRONG does not endorse the content. Rachel Armbruster was an employee at the Lance Armstrong Foundation from 2000 to 2006 but is not currently a LIVESTRONG employee and does not represent LIVESTRONG or its views; the opinions and recollections belong solely to Rachel Armbruster.

For general information on our other products and services or for technical support, please contact our Customer Care Department within the United States at (800) 762–2974, outside the United States at (317) 572–3993, or fax (317) 572–4002.

Wiley also publishes its books in a variety of electronic formats. Some content that appears in print may not be available in electronic books.
For more information about Wiley products, visit our web site at www.wiley.com.

Library of Congress Cataloging-in-Publication Data:

Armbruster, Rachel, 1975–
  Banding together for a cause : proven strategies for revenue and awareness generation / Rachel Armbruster. – 1
      p. cm.
  Includes index.
    ISBN 978-1-118-09736-6 (cloth); ISBN 978 1 118-18473-8 (ebk);
ISBN 978-1-118-18475-2 (ebk); ISBN 978-1-118-18474-5 (ebk)
    1. Nonprofit organizations–Management.   2. Social responsibility of business.
3. Strategic alliances (Business)   I. Title.
  HD62.6.A76 2012
  658.4′012–dc23

                                                          2011039255

Printed in the United States of America

10 9 8 7 6 5 4 3 2 1

This book is dedicated to my family. My husband Brandon who has always been my rock and my biggest fan. My children, Carter and Evan, who motivate me to be better every day and my parents, Jerry and Donna, without whom I would not have had the education, the spirit of giving back, or the confidence to pursue that which seemed impossible. I love you all.

Contents

Preface

"Yellow wakes me up in the morning.
Yellow gets me on the bike every day.
Yellow has taught me the true meaning of
sacrifice.
Yellow makes me suffer.
Yellow is the reason I'm here."

—Lance Armstrong

The wristband campaign was the official start of the transformation of the Lance Armstrong Foundation (Foundation). Initially, the brand LIVESTRONG really represented a new online resource center program within the Foundation. When we responded to Nike's original concept, we included the resource center in our plans to mobilize our constituents. Nike immediately recognized the power of LIVESTRONG and the band that was sold worldwide simply said LIVESTRONG.

If I hadn't personally been involved in the campaign, I almost wouldn't have believed how it came about and the magnitude of the changes that came with it for the organization, the people involved, and, most importantly, the cancer community. If you are working at a nonprofit today or for a company that is doing standard outreach and community relations, my guess is that you hear about these types of campaigns but can't really imagine how to make this happen at your own organization. It can sometimes be hard to even think about what the first step might be to go down this path.

This book's goal is to provide key insights, present meaningful questions to start your thinking, and some sense of the yellow wristband journey. Hopefully, these insights and memories will offer up best practices to help take your organization to the next level. You will notice that there is a process, a focus on improvement, and a passion for relationships that drive success. There should be nothing in this book that you cannot create for your own cause.

> *"Knowledge is Freedom: hide it, and it withers; share it, and it blooms."*
>
> —P. Hill

One of the wonderful things about working in the nonprofit space is the willingness of everyone to work for the greater good. We are all trying to change the world. When one group finds a program that works, it should be leveraged by others for other worthy causes. The key is to be the organization that *creates* the programs that others replicate and to only implement those ideas that make sense for your organization. Be a leader in the marketplace and be selective about how you spend your resources.

"The best businesses are those that have figured out how to combine profits, passion, and purpose."
—Tony Hsieh

While all of our organizations represent various causes, there is one thing that we all have in common and that is a desire to help people. Programs teams are able to help people through direct services, but for people in accounting, marketing, or development, it happens in the creation of campaigns; the development of partnerships that make people think and create lasting change in the world. Sometimes it is hard to connect the dots from how data entry in the donor-operations department plays into the larger mission of an organization. The wristband campaign and the opportunity it presents to share the experience both provide a very tangible way to connect. Don't neglect those chances to give back and help people.

It's important to note, when reading this book, that talking about your failures or those experiences that did not end in millions of dollars raised is a great opportunity for learning. Success is usually preceded by failure. Be willing to share both the successes and failures with others. The failure may even have more of an impact than the successful campaign stories. That is one of the main reasons I am documenting my experience with the wristband campaign here. I am hopeful that other nonprofits and companies are able to learn from the experiences contained in these pages. I hope the lessons I am sharing can help organizations to create campaigns to benefit poverty, diabetes, education, asthma, or any number of worthy causes. It's humbling to think, then, that my legacy would be about creating a world of change instead of being linked to one amazing campaign. In turn, maybe this will help you ask yourself these questions: "What is my legacy? How are others learning from my experiences? Have I made myself accessible?"

Sharing should be a part of every stage of your routine and process. Imagine a non-profit partnership director training a new member of the team. Typically, the scenario includes a 'watch and learn' comment and then the new person is left on their own to recreate that scene with other partner prospects. All the while, the new person is hoping they get the script right. What if that same partnership director prepared with the new person pre-meeting to share what they had prepared for the exchange, and then reviewed the entire exchange post-meeting. This is something development professionals apply often to major giving opportunities. When we are headed to a meeting with a potential donor, we take time to send a donor overview to our accompanying board member or executive. We talk through our recommended approach including the conversation starters, ask amounts, back-up plans, and more. Then, immediately after the meeting, we spend time talking about how the meeting went and where we were right on or how we missed the mark. When sharing your wisdom, experience, and insights, don't wait until you have checked off every box on your to do list. Sharing at every step of the campaign and partnership is valuable and can result in you achieving your goals even faster on your own.

This book is written on the principle that if you seek to help others and put relationships first, great things are possible. It is meant to help you develop the tools you need to experience your own success story. It's always so rewarding when I have shared an experience with someone or helped a client gain new clarity. The thought of being able to do this for more than one person at a time in a book was just too tempting. And, luckily, Doug Ulman and the team at LIVESTRONG have allowed me to share these experiences and the lessons learned.

You will find a variety of resources in this book. They include a list of additional resources, conversation starters, exercises, a corporate partnership program process outline, and more. My goal was to make this book both informative and actionable. You may also visit www.bandingtogetherforacause.com where you can enjoy watching various interview videos online. Alongside this book, the videos will help you learn from various members of the team that made LIVESTRONG possible. I have also included exercises, tools, and resources. You will find a range of photos on the web site covering my most memorable moments and keepsakes from my time at LIVESTRONG. I hope you enjoy my stroll down memory lane.

Now, join me in examining key elements of the LIVESTRONG campaign. When recalling my cause marketing experiences, I have worked to include not just the pieces that have worked but also those concepts or plans that were less than perfect. Sometimes you can learn more by seeing what not to do, than having a clear path laid out for you. And, while there were plenty of opportunities to modify ideas or plans, I believe the LIVESTRONG campaign was amazing and learned so much from the opportunity. I am honored and humbled to have been a part of it. I get emotional just thinking about the lives impacted and the difference we have made. It is not every day you are given an opportunity like the one with LIVESTRONG, and I don't take it for granted.

*   *   *

This story begins by focusing on the aspect of time within the LIVESTRONG campaign from 2000 to 2006. At the time of the initial conversation with Nike in January of 2004, the Foundation had experienced tremendous growth. The Ride for the Roses Weekend had grown from a cycling event that raised $250,000 to a weekend filled with events raising millions of dollars. We had successfully recruited more than a dozen members of our major giving club, the Founder's Circle, with each contributing a gift in excess of $500,000. The direct marketing campaign had been steadily increasing from 2002 when it was launched to the time of the wristband in 2004 and seemed promising for the future. We had identified merchandise as a potential new revenue source for the Foundation and were preparing to launch our own e-commerce site. The programs team was growing just as fast. We spent two years (from 2002 to 2004) refining our mission and identifying the place where we could make the most impact—cancer survivorship. Immediately following

Lance's diagnosis in 1996 he started thinking about how his life might be different after cancer—everything from his prospects of having a family to the impact on his career. He was not alone. The more we talked to the cancer community, the more we realized that there were others like him that needed help with the practical needs, and not just during treatment but in terms of the long-term effects that could play a role in a person's quality of life. We realized this is where we could make a meaningful contribution to the cancer community and began focusing on grants and programs. We were funding research and organizations providing direct services and we were preparing to launch our own online resource center to focus on cancer survivorship.

The LIVESTRONG staff had grown from three people when I started in 2000 to more than 50 employees. Our board was actively engaged and we were talking with a number of potential corporate partners at any given time about ways to expand our reach, raise funds, and drive people to our events or resources. With the introduction of the wristband idea in January of 2004, these activities did not stop or get derailed. They were just layered with a new sense of purpose. We had been given the chance of a lifetime and we weren't about to waste it. We had been working for years on building the infrastructure, the relationships, the reach, and the communication channels. Everything was ready to be activated and it was time!

Time is precious, so let's not waste any more of it. It's your turn to change the world by learning from the lessons in these pages from one of the most successful cause-marketing campaigns in history. Let's get started!

Acknowledgments

I would like to offer a special thanks to everyone that offered support to me when I suggested the idea of sharing this information with others and for participating in the research and interview process.

To the entire Lance Armstrong Foundation development team from 2000 to 2006, you were the best group of people I have ever had the pleasure to work with and I am better because of knowing each of you. Thank you to Jeff Garvey for your leadership and drive for excellence. And thanks to Scott for letting me be a part of his grand vision—it was an honor.

Thank you to the team at Wiley Publishing for being patient with me and helping each step of the way.

And, thank you to Lance Armstrong. I continue to be in awe of your passion for the cancer community and your ability to be in a million places at once. You made every moment fun and meaningful—which is not an easy task.

Banding Together for a Cause

Chapter 1

The Importance of Time in Moving Your Mission Forward

It is only fitting that an organization founded by a cyclist should be concerned about time and the opportunity it presents. After a lifetime of training, preparation, and effort, Lance's sixth Tour de France victory came down to less than a three-minute difference with his primary competitor.

In 2004, there was a pivotal moment during the Tour de France when Lance passed rival Ivan Basso in the l'Alpe d'Huez Time Trial. Going into the sixteenth Stage of the 2004 Tour, Lance Armstrong held a lead of 1:25 over the CSC team's Ivan Basso in the race for the overall title. The two had matched each other virtually pedal stroke for pedal stroke on three previous mountain stages where they had traded victories and finished at the same time, with Basso winning one and Armstrong taking the other two. Speculation ran high as to what would happen in the time trial. Who was really the stronger climber? Adding drama to the showdown was the fact that more than a million spectators crowded the legendary climb of Alpe d'Huez. Even at 5 a.m., the 9.6-mile course was packed with fans and resembled the world's largest rock concert more than an uphill time trial to a ski station. Riders in the time trial would have to endure cheers and jeers as they charged up the steep slopes. Who would win the brightest jewel in the climber's crown? At the first time check, Armstrong and Basso were just about even. Then the American started reeling the Italian in at a feverish pace. By the time check at 9.5 kilometers to go, Lance was up by 1:15, meaning he was just 45 seconds behind Basso after factoring two minutes for the time trial's staggered start. Lance caught his two-minute man with three kilometers to go. Basso tried to hold his wheel but there was no hanging onto the Yellow Jersey Express. The CSC rider lost 2:22 to Armstrong that day and Lance solidified his lead in what would become a record 6th Tour victory.[1]

★   ★   ★

When trying to create relationships like the one between Nike and the Lance Armstrong Foundation

---

[1] http://thecycologist.com/articles/the-10-most-memorable-moments-of-lances-7-tour-wins-pg117.htm

(Foundation), every minute matters. Everyone must be willing to invest time and energy in partner relationships to help them flourish. The LIVESTRONG wristband campaign did not happen overnight. Nike had been supporting the Foundation for years and slowly increased support each year. Over the years, Nike executives attended Foundation-hosted events and met survivors and their families impacted by the cause. Over the course of time, our main Nike representative had experienced a close connection to our founder, the organization, and its mission and was able to make the connection to the color yellow for the cancer community. It also took years for the Foundation to be ready to take on such an enormous campaign. Organizations interested in developing campaigns that will impact their cause for years in the future should be prepared for an extremely long sales cycle and a necessary investment of time to truly affect change.

Along with an investment of time, the *timing* of the various efforts is important. Throughout my interviews of past employees and partners, it was obvious that there was a "perfect storm" that took place in 2004 during the launch of the now-famous yellow wristband. Not only was Lance going for an unprecedented win number six in the Tour de France but it was also the year of the Olympics, a presidential election, the launch of the LIVESTRONG online resource center, the start of our government outreach and advocacy efforts, and Americans were looking for something positive during a time of war.

The Foundation was also at a critical point in our organizational maturity. What had started as a fundraising cycling event held annually in Austin by Lance's friends had become a professional operation investing millions each year in cancer survivorship. The Foundation was impacting the lives of millions of survivors. The staff had grown from three people in 2000 to more than 50 in 2004. A clear need had been identified for survivors and their loved ones after their point of diagnosis and the Foundation was supplying the resources and support for this growing population. Our programs team was engaging with non-profit organizations of every size around the country and our fundraising had exceeded $15 million a year. The LIVESTRONG Resource Center was set to launch in 2004, and the Foundation was anxious to parlay Lance's fame and notoriety as a beacon of hope for survivors into the number-one resource for meaningful information and resources for the cancer community. We were exploring a variety of fundraising programs and revenue-diversification strategies including cause-marketing programs, national event expansion, and the launch of the Foundation merchandise efforts. The opportunity from Nike came at the right time for the organization—another component of the "perfect storm."

Are Your Policies Flexible?

The Nike relationship was an easy sell internally in 2004. In 2000, we were not raising money from cause marketing initiatives and were relying solely on unsolicited revenue that resulted from Lance's book, *It's Not About the Bike*, and income from the annual Ride for the Roses cycling event. As the Foundation became more active in the cancer community and built its own following, the assets of the Foundation became more valuable and a cause-related marketing partnership seemed like it would have validity on its own, regardless of Lance's personal participation. When working to expand and diversify the revenue of your organization, be prepared to provide countless examples of programs or initiatives that have been successful. With thorough research and creative thinking, you will uncover the key messaging points that will inspire your board of directors and others to take action and try something new. But don't just present the facts. Introduce your leadership and board members to companies and charities that have successfully launched cause-marketing campaigns, or whatever you are trying to initiate. Facilitate the conversations that will allow them to learn for themselves that these efforts have resulted in a win for all involved parties. In 2001, the board approved the removal of the ban on cause marketing and we were able to pursue those relationships with our current and prospective partners. We were actively looking for companies that had a shared interest in making a difference in the lives of cancer survivors. We first looked to add cause-marketing partnerships to our existing relationships and we began working with companies to create mutually beneficial partnerships. A word of caution— there is a difference in not limiting yourself and allocating resources including people, time, and money. At the time we lifted the ban on cause marketing, we did not immediately hire a cause-marketing director and plan on making that a focus for our 2001 fundraising strategy. Rather, we opened the door to the possibility with existing partners and began integrating the concept into our on-going conversations. And, these were the humble beginnings of the LIVESTRONG wristband campaign.

In the past two years, I have worked with a variety of clients and occasionally I come across a situation where the organization had set policies in place that prohibit or restrict participation and giving by a specific audience. I believe the goal of every development director should be to establish channels of giving for every interested person or organization. This does not mean an organization should say yes to every proposal that comes through the door. It does mean that if someone wants to get involved and is passionate for your cause, leave no stone unturned and find a way to make their philanthropy profitable for your organization. Usually the things that are included in these rejection clauses are the things that the organization is not familiar with or that they have not experienced before. By not leaving the organization open to exploring the possibilities with a given entity, the cause and those it serves can potentially miss out on something that could be culture-shifting, such as the LIVESTRONG wristband campaign. Imagine if the Susan G. Komen Foundation for the Cure had decided it was not going to host events and set a policy in the by-laws to that effect? What if any major medical institution in the world determined that naming opportunities were not a valuable way to raise funds for their facility? The end result of these policies is that the constituents lose. There would not be the amazing medical institutions we have available to us today. Hundreds of thousands of women would be going without their annual mammograms and breast cancer research would still be an after-thought and millions of mothers, daughters, sisters, and friends would have been lost to the disease.

If the Foundation had chosen to focus only on event revenue to support the Foundation's mission, millions of cancer survivors might still be waiting for that one galvanizing moment that allowed them to say to the world: "We deserve better." While these revenue-generating opportunities may seem a little scary at first, there are plenty of examples of organizations raising significant dollars from these programs. The American Lung Association, Arthritis Foundation, and several green charities have been successful working with their partners to create programs that are meaningful to everyone, most especially the organization's constituents. You can learn from them and determine the applicability to your cause. I strongly encourage organizations to remove restrictions on revenue programs. If structured correctly and with best intentions by both parties, there are an infinite number of ways to make money for your cause. Why limit yourself before you even get started?

"When your every thought and your every action is directed to your ultimate life goals, you become unstoppable and assured of great success and happiness."
—Robin S. Sharma

Be strategic about what you go after proactively and what you are sufficiently prepared to manage reactively. Are your policies and guidelines stated? Do they prevent you from taking advantage of opportunities that can positively influence the organization? What changes should be made? What is the modification process? You are the internal champion for this change, so determine what recommendations should be made and then work diligently to impact the organizational structure so that it affords you the opportunity to pursue every revenue stream available.

Embracing Growth through Experience

What I believe is one of the most important lessons of the wristband campaign, if not THE most important thing to remember, is that the yellow wristband campaign was not the first time the Foundation and Nike had worked together. It was the culmination of years of work and partnership. When I started in 2000, Nike was providing in-kind merchandise to support our Peloton Project, which was our primary source of revenue for the Foundation. The Peloton Project members were the top 10 percent of our annual cycling event participants and they were raising 80 percent of the revenue. Our Nike representative made it a point to attend events. He used the time to get to know the staff and volunteers. He lost close family members to cancer and was personally an active supporter of our mission.

The relationship and mutual understanding of each other's organizations did not happen overnight. And, it was not something that could have been sped up for the sake of a campaign. It took time. It took a willingness, on behalf of both parties, to make the relationship a priority and invest the time to really grow together and evolve. Because of the size of the Foundation in those early years when we were 10 employees or less, we each had an opportunity to build relationships with our partners and supporters. We knew our top fund-raisers by their first names and knew all about their children, careers, and their motivation for being involved with the Foundation. Having the ability to dedicate this time to your relationships can be influenced by several factors. Key questions to ask yourself include:

- Is your organization structured in a way that not only permits employees to spend time with partners but encourages it?
- Do you have key touch points throughout the year allowing you to get to know each other?
- Are your employees given feedback during annual reviews about not only the money raised but the relationships established and fostered with an understanding for what that might lead to down the road?
- Are relationships evaluated on how they might be leveraged to impact the mission?

Having the right people in the right place at the right time is not easy to do. It is not always something you can engineer. I have definitely seen instances when relationship building was not only unsupported, but the systems and infrastructure in place actually prohibited it. Make sure you remove any roadblocks to these critical relationship-building opportunities as a first step. Then spend time thinking about the relationship network for each member or the team. Who are the relationship managers of your most valuable relationships and how are you stewarding and cultivating those individuals currently? Diligently thinking about others and determining the most effective way to serve the organization by fostering these relationships is invaluable.

In 2000, the Foundation was a small but mighty team of three. It included Bianca Bellavia, Meghan Helmbrecht, and me. We each had a fundraising and development background mixed with some marketing and communications experience. Many nonprofit organizations are unwilling to invest in the fundraising team as a start-up for fear that that the constituents and their nonprofit peers will feel like the organization is being greedy or trying to run before it can walk. In the case of the Lance Armstrong Foundation, our board was made up of venture capitalists and entrepreneurs. There was a healthy understanding that without the funding, the Foundation would not be able to make a meaningful impact. We needed to be positioned to not only capture the incoming unsolicited donations that were a result of Lance's first book, *It's Not About The Bike*, but also proactively raise funds for our mission and create new revenue streams. The board also realized the need to devote resources to our programs department as the size and volume of our grants continued to expand. The fourth hire was Doug Ulman, who began as the director of programs and is now serving as the president and chief executive officer (CEO) of the Foundation.

Over the four years prior to the launch of the wristband campaign, the organization went through many structural and leadership changes. We recruited a few executive directors with extensive non-profit backgrounds and began to grow the Foundation's team. Everyone working at the Foundation felt this overwhelming sense of opportunity and potential. I remember some of our first planning sessions when we would discuss the strengths of the Foundation and inevitably, everyone would say "our potential." And it was true—we all knew something great was going to happen and we were glad to be a part of it in the making. We worked diligently to capture everything that would impact the organization in a meaningful way. While not always pleasant, the growing pains we experienced in the early years of the Foundation were necessary.

We came to realize that we needed to focus on cancer survivorship and not just cancer. While it seemed like a small distinction to most, it was a huge turning point in the future of the Foundation. We were immediately able to focus on our core constituents and felt that other organizations were better equipped to deal with issues like prevention and screenings. These organizational changes and evolution gave us an opportunity to work more closely as a team. We were given opportunities to lead within our individual areas of responsibility and a group of directors. This sense of team became essential to the success of the wristband campaign.

> *"Boldly walk into tomorrow with a purpose and a vision for a better world."*
> —Henry Leo Bolduc

Any time you experience conflict, embrace the opportunity to learn and grow together as a team.

From the beginning there were many moving parts of the organization, and it demanded a lot from those involved. Having been through the fire together as a team made us stronger. It would have been impossible to accomplish so much in so little time without the team that made up the Lance Armstrong Foundation in 2004.

In 2002, one of our founders, Jeff Garvey, took on the role of executive director as a volunteer. He led our team for two years. He was in the office every day working side by side with us to affect change. His background at Austin Ventures, passion for the cancer cause, and ability to cut to the quick and see things differently had a profound impact. His time with the Foundation helped shape it. I attribute much of our success and Nike's interest in us as an organization to Jeff's direct involvement. He gave our young but eager staff time to mature and gain focus. He also helped us celebrate our accomplishments along the way. The executive committee of the board and the management team used these years to create infrastructure and better articulate our operations and procedures. We refined our revenue programs and began seeking revenue-diversification opportunities. We did this while maintaining and nurturing our existing fundraisers and long-time supporters.

In addition to Jeff, the Foundation was blessed with other amazing advisors. In 2003, we spent time discussing the revenue opportunities with our internal fundraising team and board fundraising and development committee. At the time, Mike Sherwin was the Development Committee Chairperson of the Lance Armstrong Foundation Board. Mike is an idea man.

Mike could always be counted on to see the possibilities and encourage the staff to examine and filter
the concepts. He also understood that not every idea
was the perfect fit. He was always willing to assess the
ideas and help us act on the best ones. Because of
the team in place on the staff, the group of advisors
on the board, and the unbelievable support from
the cancer community, the Foundation was blessed
with many opportunities for growth even prior to
the LIVESTRONG wristband campaign. Discussions
included the potential of launching a national ride
series based on the success of the Ride for the Roses,
our annual cycling event. We were talking about a
speaker's bureau and other ways to impact the organization in both awareness and revenue. In 2003, we
also begin conversations about launching a year-round
merchandise program.

Every year, during Ride for the Roses, the Foundation would have a merchandise booth at the Health
& Sports Expo. Because we were a grassroots effort
and it was a time for all hands on deck, I had recruited
my parents, Gerald and Donna Kubicki. They served
as our Merchandise Chairpeople. They had been
McDonald's owner/operators for more than 20 years
and I felt they knew a thing or two about merchandising, moving people quickly, and bookkeeping. We
sold Ride for the Roses jerseys, t-shirts, commemora-
tive posters, and other miscellaneous merchandise. We
typically sold out in 48 hours and it became a good
revenue generator inside an already successful weekend
filled with activities.

We received requests from cyclist and cancer survivors around the world to sell Ride for the Roses

Weekend and Lance Armstrong Foundation-branded merchandise year-round. We assessed the issue of cannibalizing the Ride Weekend merchandise revenue but quickly realized that in-store sales across the country would provide additional awareness of the cause along with the funding. Our first pilot was to work with Trek dealers to sell the cycling gear in their reseller outlets. The merchandise was moving successfully and we felt that we could accelerate the process by offering the merchandise online. Just prior to the wristband campaign, our development team had started building an online store to raise additional funds and awareness for the Foundation through the sale of Ride for the Roses branded merchandise and products geared toward helping cancer survivors. The development team began seeking out experts in online merchandising and fulfillment.

We knew launching something like this would require us to pull from experts in the field and had hoped to build our knowledge of the process as we went. One of our board members connected us with one of his former students, who ran an Austin-based fulfillment company. He was immediately on board and helped teach our team about logistics, online stores, customer service, operations, and more. We also started working with consultants who had retail and buying experience. Every step of the way, we kept informing Nike of our new plan and expressed our interest in their involvement as either a supplier or partner. Nike had provided much of the merchandise for the Ride Weekend sales and we knew their involvement could ensure success.

Generating Big Ideas

By this time, the organization had diversified its revenue to include direct marketing, major giving, events, merchandise, cause marketing, and grants. In January, we were busy building the store and executing our 2004 fundraising plan. That same month, I received a call from Bill Stapleton, Lance's agent. Bill said that Scott was flying in from Nike and wanted to meet with our President and CEO and me. We met at Bill's office. I knew we were in for something special when our Nike representative presented a slide deck for us to review. Typically our meetings were casual conversations and focused on logistics for upcoming activities and events. I was very curious. Our contact explained the development of a "simple big idea." He walked us through his presentation. He showed us the wristband concept and the campaign overview. On the cover of his presentation was an image of Lance and the headline "Yellow Fever Hits America." At the end of his pitch, he had a question for us. He wanted to know how we planned to mobilize our growing community of supporters. He needed to know if we had the capabilities in place to determine the distribution mechanism for five million wristbands. And finally, what would we do with the resulting funds?

Our President and I returned to the office with the presentation and gathered the management and development team. We walked them through the opportunity. Our conversation quickly shifted to our existing programs and initiatives. We needed to determine how they might best be applied to making this campaign come to life. I called key members of our board and shared the news. I left those conversations with another set of questions for the internal team. One initial response to the idea was, "We'll sell more than five million." You had to love the optimism.

The recently established merchandise team was engaged in the process. We shifted our conversations from selling branded cycling gear to wristband sales and fulfillment. I truly believe that our willingness to diversify revenue and think about social-venture opportunities prior to 2004 made the organization more attractive to partners. It allowed companies to think about us not only as a charity partner, but as a true business partner capable of solving business operations issues and capturing marketing opportunities. We were asking the right questions in our meetings with partners and we were headed down the right path. Our partners were eager to help us succeed and they saw that timing was right—including Nike.

Recognizing Your Time as a Valuable Resource

Time is also important because it is something everyone has to be willing to give up to really make a difference. In order to implement new campaigns, build relationships, and ensure your organization is relevant to those it serves, you must be willing to contribute your time and energy to the mission of the organization. Ideas do not often get hand delivered to you like the presentation from Nike was, complete with a yellow ribbon—or wristband in this case. Usually the ideas are a little rough around the edges and it will take time to outline the specifics and evaluate the opportunity. You will have to work to make the final concept ready for its intended audiences. In *The Elegant Solution*[2] by Matthew E. May, he talks about The Da Vinci Dilemma:

> "Leonardo da Vinci was never at a loss for big ideas. Brilliant, ingenious ideas centuries before their time filled the pages of his legendary notebooks. And that's where they remained. Until the innovators in another lifetime took them and shaped them into something actually workable. . . . And the earth-shattering ideas are few and far between. They have huge lead times. They have enormous carrying costs. You absolutely need them to pepper the advance into new eras of industry. But for the mainstream business that seeks to achieve and sustain continuous success through steady progress, the real power of innovation lives in the minor tremors—the more plentiful and more immediately actionable smaller ideas."

When someone has an idea, do not immediately dismiss it because it seems too grand or overwhelming. Dedicate the time and work to refine and scale the idea. Talk about the possibilities of piloting the program. Do your due diligence to ensure its success before charging full steam ahead. Never dismiss an idea outright. You and your team have to be willing to

---

[2] *The Elegant Solution*. Matthew E. May. Free Press, New York, October 10, 2006.

invest the time in the discussions and allow yourselves to talk about the potential. Then you can make informed decisions and plan accordingly. Not every partnership will be the big one and not every campaign can be the tipping point for your organization. Be willing to take those first steps. Take time to make those tremors happen and know that they are all leading to something great. The investment of time will be worth it and you never know when an idea you spent time discussing two years ago will all of a sudden become relevant again with some new piece of information.

Along with allowing yourself and your team time to think about the possibilities, you need to allow time for objectively examining opportunities and existing programs. Make sure you are routinely reviewing the numbers from current programs and take the time to forecast potential new endeavors. If this is a standard part of your team's activities, you will be more likely to make informed and relevant decisions. Use these opportunities throughout the year to create relationships with your internal resources. Interactions with your finance, marketing, and programs teams for these assessment conversations will be educational across departments. You will have a better understanding of what the priorities are for each department and be better positioned to address their needs and concerns in the future. You will also have a much easier conversation internally when an opportunity comes available and there is a short timeline involved. People will be willing to rally and give you their time and make the impossible happen.

Be conservative with how and when you ask for favors or look to leverage these relationships. Only apply time pressure when it is in the best interest of the organization and when the impact is going to be substantial. When working on partnerships, immediate action is not always a good thing. Rushing something that needs time to develop can cause a really great idea to fail in execution. Be sure that during your planning process you take the time to review historical data and look back on past experiences. Don't rely solely on this data but rather use it to help avoid mistakes previously made and let it help guide the new plan. If you are not sure what data points to consider, get outside suggestions. Let others provide input on what to collect. Ask peers, mentors, colleagues, and others what questions they would ask when evaluating this relationship and you will learn what to collect and review for your own assessment. Working with your finance team can help you run the numbers and make sure you are all aware of the potential impact to the bottom line.

Another important factor to take the time to consider is the intangible benefit your organization will receive from the opportunity. Intangibles can include exposure to your audiences, feature stories in national communication materials, hospitality opportunities, and the potential to serve on program-input groups and committees. Occasionally we would compromise on our impact standards for a corporate agreement because we felt our willingness to be flexible would pay off in the long term with the partner. Determine your absolute boundaries. Do not put the organization in a situation that results in a net loss but never be afraid to invest in relationships with people and organizations that are mission-motivated and have assets that can be leveraged for your cause. Time is a limited and precious resource and you make a choice every minute of how you will spend that resource—choose wisely.

Knowing Yourself and Your Constituents

Another investment of time occurs with knowing your constituents. Who do you have the honor and privilege of representing? We will discuss this more deeply during the branding chapter, but it is worth noting that investing time in knowing your audience, empathizing with them, and understanding what will truly help them will allow you to better position the organization with your partners. Your intimate knowledge of this audience will help ensure that every partnership deal will make a true impact. It is our responsibility as stewards of our cause to educate those interested in helping and take the time to develop meaningful programs and fundraising campaigns. This ability to share insights about the audience comes from spending time with those you represent.

Listening to your customers and constituents is not something that can be rushed or done halfway. It has to be a real priority for every member of the team. The leadership of the organization should lead by example. If the CEO and other executives spend less than 5 percent of their time interacting and listening to the organization's customers and those they serve, it sends a message to the rest of the company. That message is that the work of the organization can be done in a bubble. And that customer input is not a necessity to completing the work. It means that constituent input, relations, and knowledge of your audience is not necessary in order to complete the job to the best of their abilities.

Make the time to get to know your audience. Even if those around you aren't currently making it a priority, you will be amazed at how quickly others will notice the difference in your quality of work, relevance of ideas, and potential for long-lasting and direct impact. If you are new to an organization, there is no time like the present to educate yourself and become acquainted with those most directly involved in the cause. If you are in a position to impact training and education processes, be sure to discuss the potential for training and exposure to your core audience. Providing these touch points regularly will keep people motivated, generate new ideas, and ensure that your organization is in touch with the needs and desires of your clients.

> *"If I have the belief that I can do it, I shall surely acquire the capacity to do it, even if I do not have it at the beginning."*
> —Mahatma Gandhi

Spending time with your primary audience is an applicable lesson for charity professionals and those working at for-profit businesses. Every person has 24 hours in a day. It is important to examine the end result of the time you are spending and the activities you are choosing to focus on. Did your 24 hours make an impact? In hundreds of cause-marketing offices around the country, people are spending time on very low-producing programs—programs that won't really register with their constituents and that won't move either organization forward. This is a choice and a decision—often without consideration for the alternatives. We all have the same amount of time and we need to be very conscious of how we use this precious resource. Comedian and philosopher Steven Wright once said, "Everywhere is within walking distance, if you have the time!" In *Creating Relational Capital*[3], John Holland and Ed Wallace expounded on this and said, "Everywhere was within walking distance because I made the time." Be sure you are making the time to achieve the goals you have set for yourself, the organization, and your partners.

Prioritizing Your Time

Another essential element when considering time is prioritization. I am a huge fan of making to-do lists. I have stacks of composition notebooks with to-do lists. I have always enjoyed that feeling of checking things off the list.

As a development director and someone responsible for generating revenue, I always felt that my to-do

---

[3] *Creating Relational Capital*. John Holland and Ed Wallace. The Relational Capital Group, Inc., Newton Square, PA, August 30, 2007.

lists were mostly about management tasks or TPS reports and less about engaging donors in the work we were doing. One simple solution was to put a dollar sign next to every action item that would generate a contribution, big or small, for the Foundation. That was my prioritization—my filter. I didn't prioritize the rest of the list—just the ones related to my success with fundraising or something that would help one of my team members raise a dollar. Sometimes this was a catch-up call with a donor and at other times it was direct solicitation. But any action that would result in funding for the mission of the Foundation would get the $ and those would be the first items checked off the list. This way, even if I ended up dealing with emergencies in the afternoon, I would know that my morning was productive and that I had contributed to the overall annual goals of my team and the organization. When trying to prioritize your task lists, a few helpful questions to ask include:

- How are you currently prioritizing the action items you have on your list? Do you sort them by type of task, the source of the task, or by deadline or due date? Is your prioritization technique a reflection of your organizational, departmental, or individual contribution goals?
- Do you wait for someone else to prioritize the list for you? If so, what piece of information or key insights will give you the information you need to prioritize on your own? Getting this information will give you the confidence to know that the items you choose to focus on will be meaningful to the organization and your leadership.

- What is most important for you to focus on today, tomorrow, in five weeks? Using your calendar online is a great way to set reminders for longer-term projects or tasks and remove them from your current to-do list. No point in cluttering it up.
- If you are not in a fundraising role within the organization, what is your equivalent to the dollar sign as a prioritization tool? What are some easy indicators for your task lists that will allow you to be more deliberate with how you spend your time?
- How realistic is your current list of to-do items? If I begin to feel like things are getting a little hectic and I am overwhelmed by my never-ending to-do list, I will start each morning with a fresh piece of paper and will write my top four or five tasks for the day. Sometimes I find that I can only accomplish the first three but it helps me stay focused and feel a sense of accomplishment at the end of the day. It is also a great filtering tool because it is amazing the number of items that will never be transferred to future versions.
- What can you delegate? What items are currently on your list that shouldn't have been there in the first place? This is for all tasks and is not relegated to internal resources. What items are on your to-do list that could be more effectively handled externally? Can you use your to-do lists to help outline a potential job description and are you looking for trends in the type of work or knowledge necessary to complete tasks? You can use your to-do lists to help make a case for additional resources. You can also use previous task lists to

clearly articulate what type of help is needed and identify trends regarding spikes in activity throughout the year.

· What should your to-do list look like in order to give you the best chance for success?

Respecting Other People's Time

When you are assessing a potential campaign concept, evaluate the amount of time each audience will need to invest to make the campaign effective. This includes the time needed from your marketing and communications team to get a program or campaign out in the public eye. Evaluate the time required from your volunteers to share the message or sign up for activation activities. A cause-marketing program may not be as successful if it requires a 10-minute sign-up process online or if you are asking each of your supporters to spend valuable time filling out and mailing in forms to capture a one-dollar donation from a partner. When running the numbers and assessing the value of the program, both tangibles and intangibles, be sure to include the time you, your team, your volunteers, and your constituents will invest. Along with valuing your mission, your partner should value your time and the time of those you represent. Use time as a filter on your campaign concepts and execution plans. Be aware not only of how you are spending your time, but also how you are asking others to spend theirs.

★   ★   ★

Time continues to be a critical factor in the success and growth of the organization. In 2005, the innovation department was working on several new ideas that have come to life in the past 12 to 24 months at the Foundation. Randall Macon, former director of innovation at LIVESTRONG stated, "You can't just look at the band campaign and say 'that just happened.' You have got to be thinking about things years in advance because they don't just magically happen." This was applicable to every aspect of the campaign, including the creation of the brand LIVESTRONG.

There was an evolution of the brand that took time and was not something that could be forced or rushed. While we had talked about needing change, it wasn't until 2003 that the pieces started to fall into place. We had always been diligent stewards of Lance's brand and took great care in how we used the Foundation's name given that it was a direct reflection of our namesake. When the cancer community connected with the LIVESTRONG brand, we had to become very deliberate with our use of the brand because it was no longer a brand associated with one individual—LIVESTRONG was a brand created by and for the cancer survivorship community. This was not a responsibility we took lightly. In the next chapter, we will discuss the evolution of the brand, its importance during the campaign, and its lasting impact for the organization.

Chapter 2

Reflecting the Essence and Spirit of Your Organization through Branding

The Lance Armstrong Foundation (Foundation) name reflects the essence and spirit of the brand, both as the Lance Armstrong Foundation and as LIVESTRONG. Attributes that come to mind when I hear the name Lance Armstrong include fighter, champion, entrepreneur, family man, demands excellence, loyal, friend, and inquisitive. The brand LIVESTRONG was originally intended to be the name of a specific program at the Foundation. In 2004 we were launching the new online resource center for cancer survivors and we were seeking a brand for that resource. Through a series of conversations internally and with Nike, it became apparent that LIVESTRONG was the brand that should be emblazoned on the wristbands.

LIVESTRONG served as both a brand and a rally cry at the same time. It was also a term that lent itself to viral marketing. This was a key component to the success of the campaign because the Foundation did not have a budget allocated to marketing and communications of the wristband. We relied solely on Nike's marketing support and our ability to utilize grassroots marketing. Any investment we made in mass media with billboards and print could not compete with people wearing the band and talking about it, at school, at work, at church, in the home—everywhere. The grassroots network was our true marketing asset.

The LIVESTRONG brand will live on long after any one individual and will continue to serve the Foundation for years to come. The brand creation and dissemination is a lasting legacy that can be attributed to a select group of individuals. But the name did not come immediately during the first brainstorming session. There was a process involved that required many hours of research, focus testing, and intense scrutiny of whether or not it captured the spirit of Lance, those he represented, and their fight against cancer.

Finding the Perfect Name

The resource center leadership team, Randall Macon and Tiffany Galligan, had gone through extensive branding efforts to select the name LIVESTRONG. They worked with a local marketing and communications agency to find a name that truly represented the spirit and attitude of the organization and the program they were championing. Everything about the online resource center was meant to be focused on the individual cancer survivors going through their journeys.

There was a great deal of energy put into making the resource center intuitive. Randall and Tiffany had spent days watching survivors navigate the internet searching for information or listening to them talk with one another to understand the types of issues and concerns that were most interesting to the community. The goal was not to create another list of resources but rather to serve as an online community where you could ask questions, find answers, and talk about issues that were relevant to your given situation. The Foundation was not interested in duplicating the efforts of government resources or other nonprofit organizations. Through our research, we had found that cancer survivors felt that only one part of the cancer journey was being openly discussed and that was related to medical information. Our new online resource center focused on the practical tools and information. This included things like insurance, how to talk with your children about being diagnosed, fertility concerns, preparing for end of life, exercise while going through treatment, career challenges, and more. We wanted to get into the details with people and felt this was a way to really change the way people approached their treatment and this would improve their quality of life beyond cancer. Taking this information and new approach, Randall and Tiffany worked with the agency to find a name that would embody the innovation of this new program.

The marketing agency started the process by learning as much as possible about the Foundation and the new resource center. They spoke with survivors, reviewed other nonprofit resources, and talked with the Foundation staff extensively. There was a sense that cancer survivors felt like they belonged to a tribe, they were a connected group and the name and logo of the program should represent that. At the same time, we were gaining credibility in the medical field and needed to label the resource center in a way that would resonate with healthcare professionals and that medical institutions and other cancer groups would be able to identify with. After several rounds of review, a decision was made to move forward with "This Point Forward." The marketing team went back to the office to celebrate, but later shared that the name was not a fit. Their CEO referred back to Lance's first book and found a passage that stated "Fight like hell." She compared this to the new name of the resource center and she realized the name wasn't right. After a discussion with the team at the Foundation and everyone in agreement that we still weren't quite there, they returned with LIVESTRONG. The original logo looked like two interlocked C's which made up the S. It looked tribal. It made a statement. It sounded like something you would want to hear at the point of diagnosis. It felt like Lance. It captured the essence of our founder, the organization, and the community we proudly served. The branding team relied on a touchstone to determine the fit and appropriateness of the final name. The team asked themselves, "Does the name convey the brand essence or Lance's 'fight like hell' attitude?" Other brand options did not meet the same approval and acceptance as LIVESTRONG. We knew we had found something special.

Our vendor's dedication to find the perfect name and not just something that would suffice was impressive and a lesson to be learned. It connected everything about our founder, how the organization was evolving, and how the Foundation wanted people to approach a cancer diagnosis.

> *"A string is needed to gather scattered beads."*
> —African Proverb

The logo of the Foundation has continued to evolve over time. In the case of LIVESTRONG, it was important that the brand represented the people the Foundation serves. Organizations named after a specific person can be difficult because often people have unrealistic expectations of appearances or involvement. By focusing on who your Foundation is helping instead of who founded the organization, you may alleviate some of these challenges later on.

It is always important to know your core assets and brand attributes. Lance and the color yellow were critical to the success of the wristband campaign. The image of the bike and the name LIVESTRONG were both manifestations of Lance's never give up attitude and his ability to overcome. We needed to embrace them both and once the Foundation made this realization, it began to move forward in a much stronger and bolder direction.

Refining the Brand

Now that the brand had been launched and we felt a change was in order for the remainder of the organization we needed to bring in outside counsel. The next step in our branding process was to engage a marketing firm in New York. They worked to further develop the brand. The original logo of the intertwined C's seemed to get lost after the image of the wristband emerged. Another change was that the original LIVESTRONG logo was orange so it was also revised to be consistent with the new efforts to make yellow the color representing cancer survivorship. The new look and feel was meant to set the Foundation apart from the other cancer organizations in the marketplace. When doing branding research for your organization, make a special note of what other brands in your space tend to look like. When seeing all of the logos together on one page, you will notice that the logos, images, and colors are all very muted and the people were always smiling and happy or just the opposite. Determine the right fit for your community. The research we reviewed allowed us to see that there was an opportunity for the Foundation's brand to stand out amongst the crowd and truly represent the cancer survivorship community. The end result of a color pallet based on black, yellow, and white provided a very straightforward type treatment for the logo and helped the Foundation stand out in the cancer community visually. While the logo refinements were essential and have remained consistent for the past few years, the biggest

"An elegant solution is quite often a single tiny idea that changes everything."

—Matthew E. May

takeaway from our work with this agency was the LIVESTRONG manifesto.

I remember hearing the manifesto for the first time and getting shivers. We were sitting in a board room with our management team and board of directors. When the account team finished reading it to the group, Lance smiled. Everyone in the room knew we were listening to something that would resonate with tens of millions of survivors and quickly help people understand who we are, what we stood for, and that we weren't taking a back seat. It was so strong and powerful. It allowed everyone involved with the organization to put to rest any lingering doubt about the name of the organization, our relationship with our leader, or our fight like hell attitude. It was perfect.

Being Authentic and the Long-Term Value of Your Brand

Every organization struggles with their name and has experienced multiple revisions to their logo or messaging. The next time you are in the middle of these branding meetings and seeking names for new programs and campaigns, remember: Be who you are! Be authentic and genuine. Once we learned to embrace this, everything fell into place and there has been a consistency and pride that has come along with that realization. Being authentic is more important than brand hierarchy or logo guidelines. Be sure your name and your brand truly represent your essence and the spirit of your organization. I refer to the LIVESTRONG brand as an "elegant solution."

In the book *The Elegant Solution*,[1] Matthew E. May defines elegance:

> "Great innovation is nearly impossible without understanding and appreciating the concept of elegance as it relates to solving important problems. . . . Elegance is about finding the aha solution to a problem with the greatest parsimony of effort and expense. Creativity plays a part. Add in subtlety, economy, and quality, and you get elegance.
>
> The effects of elegant solutions are significant, ranging from understated intellectual appreciation to truly seismic change. Elegant solutions relieve creative tension by solving the problem *in finito* as it's been defined, in a way that avoids creating other problems that then need to be solved. Elegant solutions render only new possibilities to chase and exploit.
>
> Finally, elegant solutions aren't obvious, except, of course, in retrospect."

When asked about the lasting impact of the wristband campaign, Doug Ulman, chief executive officer (CEO) of LIVESTRONG, states that the greatest legacy of the partnership is the gift of this amazing brand to the organization. He provides examples of brands such as the YMCA, Girl Scouts, and American Red Cross that took 50 to 100 years to build. LIVESTRONG, a start-up organization with less than 100 employees, has been given this amazing brand. They are able to

---

[1] *The Elegant Solution*. Matthew E. May. New York, NY, Free Press, 2007.

leverage it to benefit cancer survivors around the globe. As a cancer survivor himself, he said, "If someone would've told me that I would one day wear something on my wrist everyday that outwardly showed my connection to the cancer community, I would have said no way." The Nike campaign facilitated this connection and it is the responsibility of the charity to serve as good brand stewards. Their job is to continue leveraging the brand to produce real change and impact. The Foundation has done a great job of remembering the basic concepts behind the name evolution and they have stayed true to the brand that was generated from this process. They have not sought to revise or refresh the brand but have kept it simple and pure.

Keeping It Simple

Many of those closest to the LIVESTRONG wristband campaign attribute its success to the simplicity of the original idea. In partnership with Nike, we had created a simple action, simple message, and simple donation allowing the greatest accessibility possible. From the beginning, Nike's primary interest was to create a campaign that provided the greatest amount of accessibility and allowed for global solidarity against the disease. This guided every decision including whether or not to include the Nike swoosh on the wristband. This is the type of partner you should be seeking for your cause. Not every partner will be as selfless as Nike in this instance, but when you find one, cherish it, and you will do great things together for your cause.

The Foundation sought out every possible way to leverage the campaign. The team had created a wish list of ideas and concepts to go along with the campaign. When the Foundation began trying to layer these components onto the campaign, Nike kept repeating over and over again: Keep It Simple. And, they were right. There would be plenty of time after the initial launch to work on follow-up components and new outreach efforts, but the initial concept needed to be pure and simple. The message needed to be direct and have only one call to action.

When you are building a new campaign, take the time to boil it down to one sentence. If it's complicated, it stands a greater chance of failure. Bianca said one of her key lessons from the wristband campaign was that a charity's message and brand should "hit right to the heart—directly, simply, quickly in order to cut through the clutter." This is more effective for the target audience and it is more actionable for the internal teams as well.

Integration was made easier because of the simple message. And quick integration of the LIVESTRONG wristband messaging into our events, direct marketing, advocacy, web site, and more was essential. The Tour de France began in early July and we had less than 90 days of true planning and production time. It would be a gross understatement to say that time to fully incorporate this campaign into our existing programs was short. Many charities would have struggled to execute this campaign. The Foundation was a centralized and flexible group. Organizations with extensive chapter networks or with de-centralized leadership should be sure to assess the time it will take the organization to pursue an idea like the wristband. Questions to ask include:

- Who would need to be included in conversations with the corporate partner?
- Who would serve as the point person for the account?
- How would we communicate to our internal constituents?
- What channels of communication do we have available for external communications to our first tier of supporters and partners?

Along with a simple message, operationalizing a campaign requires a strong team. It not only requires full support from marketing and development, but all other support services including technology, human resources, and operations.

Positioning Your Brand as an Authority

Another valuable outcome from the wristband campaign and from the creation of the brand LIVESTRONG was the ability of the organization to position itself as a cancer authority. Through the research conducted during the creation of the online resource center, we knew that the cancer community connected with Lance the survivor and Lance the athlete. Although this connection was strong and provided a source of hope and inspiration, these same individuals did not acknowledge Lance, or his Foundation, as the primary source of information or authority about cancer survivorship. Prior to 2004 and the development of the LIVESTRONG brand, it was hard to imagine how we could bridge that gap. We needed to find a way to effectively position the Foundation as a trusted source of cancer information. At the same time, trying to promote other personalities, besides Lance, within the organization as authorities on given topics had been previously unsuccessful because of the Foundation's name and the expectation of Lance's personal involvement.

Many athlete foundations focus on fundraising and utilizing their celebrity status to further any number of causes. Occasionally, these same organizations have directly offered services to a group of constituents and become a major player in their given cause. At the Lance Armstrong Foundation, we were founded by an athlete that wanted to do things differently. He was not satisfied with the resources, research, and current approach to cancer. He knew that it could and should be done differently. Lance sought to build a team of advisors that would help him identify a larger group of motivated individuals that could make his vision a reality.

One meaningful step toward establishing itself as the go-to cancer organization was the creation and proliferation of the LIVESTRONG brand. In a matter of months, LIVESTRONG became the authority on all things survivorship. This allowed the organization to have a greater impact on its constituents. It is important to realize that the marketing campaign alone would not have been enough. There had to be substance behind the name. The work that had been done by the Foundation in the years leading up to the

LIVESTRONG campaign demonstrated that our team had been diligently working on behalf of the cancer-survivorship community. It sent a clear message that we were the right organization to address their unmet needs. The opportunity to immediately direct people to the online resource center and the launch of our phone-based patient-navigation services provided scalable and informative channels of communication. We had developed the resources over the last few years, but, until the wrsitband campaign, we struggled to reach each individual at the point of diagnosis and affect real change.

We felt a need to reach out and be in front of the patient at this pivotal moment in their cancer journey. The LIVESTRONG wristband changed this entire model. After the wristband launched, newly diagnosed survivors and their loved ones would call the Foundation within their first few phone calls. This type of reach was such a gift. The acceptance and approval from a programmatic standpoint from the cancer community was overwhelming.

Recognizing and Allowing Evolution

In the original wristband concept presentation by Nike, they stated, "This brand [Nike] has always been about the celebration of human potential. Lance articulates this better than anyone." I appreciate Nike's ability to elevate a shoe company to something that represents so much more for people—"the celebration of human

> *"We must not only give what we have, we must give what we are."*
> —Desire-Joseph Mercier

potential." Many times we wondered why Nike signed Lance as a Nike athlete all those years ago. At the time of the original endorsement, Nike was not focused on the cycling market. Prior to Lance's Tour de France wins there was not much interest in him as an athlete endorser and he was better known overseas where cycling was more prevalent. We gained additional insight into the reasoning behind their decision when we read that line from the presentation. It was then very clear. Nike chose Lance, not because of his abilities on the bike, but because he was a perfect example of what is possible. Watching Lance overcome such an incredible athletic challenge and his determination and willingness to accept nothing less than perfection cause us all to examine our own application of our human potential. It is motivating and humbling all at once.

Nike's ability to focus on the larger picture and meaning of Lance gave the Foundation team the freedom to make the brand changes we all knew should happen. A simple but meaningful brand change would not disassociate us from Lance, but would take the best brand attributes from Lance and combine them with a brand that could offer expert opinions and services to our constituents. Up to this point, we had been hesitant to implement a complete brand shift for fear of alienating those we had already connected with. But we were short-sighted and did not see the potential of mobilizing our current support base while attracting a whole new group of motivated individuals.

Thinking back to the evolution of the name and identity, I realize how many versions of the Lance

Armstrong Foundation we asked our community to embrace. We had distinct logos for events, programs, and campaigns. In some cases, it was difficult to tell if we were representing the Foundation, the American Cancer Society, or any number of other organizations. At times we were more interested in creating brands that could be leveraged in collateral materials and in advertising than a brand that connected with our constituents. This line of thinking was flawed. We had a desire to give sponsors an opportunity to buy in to specific brands thinking this was the end goal. In reality, corporate partners are not interested in the brand identity, but rather the people that the brand represents. Originally the brand was about the founder of the organization. Then the sub-brands became about the programs they represented. It wasn't until 2004 and the transition to LIVESTRONG that the brand truly represented the cancer community.

There are so many brands in the world that do not resonate with their core customers or constituents. These brands don't motivate. They aren't life changing. Other brands, brands that do connect, can change the world. This is more important than ever for charity brands because of the lack of marketing dollars and resources. A strong brand can transcend normal communication channels and become part of the fabric of society. This is what companies and individuals want to associate with—to be a part of. When a brand like this is in your care, you must be diligent about the use of the brand and how you leverage and share it. And remember that what you do and don't do with the brand is equally important. We needed to be sure about the partners we did work with and understand how they fit into our culture, organization, and how our association would positively impact the cancer community. Sometimes what you say no to is more important than what you end up doing.

Building and Maintaining Brand Ownership

In 2004, we made significant branding changes that allowed us to evolve into an organization that served millions instead of hundreds of thousands. There was a simplicity to the brand that was very powerful. The call to action in those days was simple: Wear Yellow. LIVESTRONG. Everyone felt a sense of ownership of the brand. The company responsible for helping to create LIVESTRONG refers to the brand as one that builds community. The agency's president and founder defines brand as a collection of the perceptions associated with you. Often times, brands are constructed with a top-down approach. The organization builds and maintains ownership of the brand. Occasionally, the organization will share it with its constituents and partners. This fundamentally limits the growth of the brand and the organization it represents. The truly meaningful brands are ones that belong to the people the organization serves; they are entangled in people's lives and relationships. These brands support and truly represent communities, not just serve them. Organizations must ask themselves about the accessibility of their brand.

- Is your brand accessible?
- Do those you serve readily associate themselves with you?

- Do you enable your community to share your brand and message freely?
- Do you place barriers in the way of spreading real awareness and change?

"The images you send out about yourself into the world determine how other people see you."
—Sanaya Roman

Because of the evolution of social media and the ability for everyone to create marketing collateral and event signage from their home computers, protecting a brand is no longer a viable option. This is not intended to mean that you ignore blatant fraud issues or don't address problems when the brand is being used in an unflattering way. It does mean you should provide the tools and resources for people to use the brand and connect with the organization. If you do not provide the resources, they will end up figuring it out on their own and you will be focused on policing the usages instead of celebrating the outcomes of those outreach opportunities. The Foundation has enabled thousands of people to connect with the LIVESTRONG brand through the creation of Team LIVESTRONG and other audience-specific brand extensions. A brand created by the community and for the community should be accessible to the community. Do not underestimate the power of grassroots marketing and do not get in its way. Be a facilitator and a resource provider and not the brand police. You can serve as an example of how the brand can best be applied and make sure that your audience has a sense for the best applications.

Doug Ulman, the CEO of LIVESTRONG, says that LIVESTRONG is a "brand created with and by survivors." This is something that is not taken lightly by those individuals who work at the Foundation. They understand that they have been given an opportunity to represent the brand and they take it very seriously.

Knowing Your Audience

The brand is one very clear and visible manifestation of the importance of knowing your audience. LIVESTRONG came from extensive research and time spent with cancer survivors. From the hours spent listening, it became apparent that our constituents desired: A better language to describe what was happening; to network and feel part of a larger community; and something that truly encompassed the entire cancer experience.

We were lucky. Lance's book made our namesake accessible. Not every organization has this asset. Take time to think about what you do have that can provide that touch stone or check point for the brand. And, remember that the final brand may not quickly resonate with everyone. LIVESTRONG was extremely polarizing in focus group testing and in some cases caused heated discussions among those being interviewed. Be comfortable with the division and be prepared to really meet the needs and interests of *your* audience—don't try to be all things to all people.

Your partners are eager for you to share your key insights and intimate knowledge about your audience with them. By showing an interest in partnership, they are acknowledging that your organization maintains a connection and a deeper understanding of the audience they are trying to appeal to or impact. There are many reasons a company will seek out charity partners. For some, it is simply the publicity or appearance of goodwill. For others, it is a way to engage their employees or customers in causes that are meaningful to them. And, in some cases, the company is interested in your audience for their corporate financial objectives. The key is to understand their goals and objectives and provide them with the knowledge they need to make the most of the partnership. Your insights about the organization's audiences are valuable assets that should be considered when evaluating the worth of the agreement to each organization. And do not limit yourself to simply your primary audience.

A sponsorship opportunity recently presented itself to my client, the Austin Film Society. The sponsor prospect was not interested in the general public and the average cinema lover. It was focused on individuals in the film industry that would potentially use their editing equipment. The communications director was able to speak effectively about the people in the filmmakers' membership group. Her intimate knowledge of the continuing education that had already been offered, where they gathered, and what they have been stating as their needs was greatly appreciated by the sponsor and they wanted to learn more. This knowledge gave them the confidence they needed to join as a corporate member and sign on as a corporate sponsor for an upcoming cast and crew screening at a summer premiere.

Be prepared to share what you know and get companies engaged in the process. If you share this knowledge, you can work together to accomplish your goals. And, audiences are getting smarter. They expect a level of sophistication from their charity partners and the companies that they associate with. Cancer survivors trust that the Foundation will only bring to the table corporate partners that may be of interest to them. Organizations will lose support quickly if they are selling their distribution lists or allowing unlimited access to donors and supporters for products and services that seem irrelevant. We can follow our donors on Facebook. We can sign up to receive their Twitter posts. This, in addition, to their personal fundraising pages for events, and click-through habits for the monthly e-newsletters, gives us no excuse for not knowing them. We should have an idea of what motivates them, their connection to the cause, and their needs and interests.

> *"Use words to change your situation, not to describe it."*
> —Lee J. Colan

Branding also requires a tremendous amount of bravery and willingness to learn as you go. You will never be able to imagine all of the places or ways your brand will be utilized. Embrace the opportunities and learn from every experience. If you are going to truly have a community brand, shared ownership is key and you must be there to support and advise but not seek to hinder and discourage. Bianca reflects on the experience and asks, "How much of this was truly in our control?" Charities and partners should be okay with this unknown and know that this is usually when real progress occurs. Organizations should be prepared to embrace this shared sense of ownership. It is perfectly reflected in the LIVESTRONG manifesto where practically every line starts with *we*. The "We" is not referring to the staff at LIVESTRONG but rather the entire cancer community—This is LIVESTRONG. Do not underestimate the power of your brand to motivate and inspire. Be thoughtful about how you share and utilize the brand and don't take it lightly.

Marketing without a Budget

A strong brand makes it easier to market without a budget. Even when an idea like the wristband is presented, it does not always result in an immediate increase in a marketing and communications budget. You have to get creative and pull together all of your assets. The Foundation turned to our partners and our community. And this ability to rally the community was a key component of the Foundation's involvement in the campaign. Nike could bring their marketing resources to the project and LIVESTRONG could compliment their efforts by mobilizing on a grassroots level. The Foundation and Nike each had a role to fill with the campaign and it would not have worked otherwise. Reflecting on this piece of the project, I realize that this was another great outcome of the wristband campaign. Up to this point, we had not galvanized or mobilized our various audience

"Don't paint stripes on your back if you're not a zebra. Focus on your unique abilities."
—Lee J. Colan

segments. The Foundation spoke to them all individually and did not have a clear message that we shared across all of the organization. This was another advantage that the organization had post–wristband. The ability to motivate the entire network of individuals and organizations was very powerful and not something every charity could successfully manage. Step one was to identify all of the various segments of our organization and then we set out to create the tools they would need to help us spread the word.

We developed a digital partner page on our web site that provided everyone with the resources and messaging they would need to support our efforts and to get involved in the campaign. The support included everything from graphics and advertising templates for both print and online to scripts and public service announcements. Instead of trying to reach out to each group individually, the creation of the partner web site made the campaign scalable. The Foundation created the resources and best practices.

Since my days at the Foundation, I have seen several organizations make a deliberate choice to keep logos and brand elements under guarded lock and key only to see some of the worst offenses occur. When people want to connect with your brand and the organization and they are not given the tools to do so, they will create their own. And, they will not always look like you would hope. Embrace the willingness to raise awareness and support for your cause and facilitate active engagement for every level of supporter. This is the only way to embrace the size and impact of your cause and to be bigger than you thought possible.

You will not be able to change lives by approving logo usage and sending out files individually. You will impact entire communities if you provide the opportunity for that community to get involved and take action. Take an assessment of where your brand falls and whether or not it is in need of change. Ask yourself and your colleagues:

- How are you leveraging your brand?
- Does your audience connect in a powerful way with your brand?
- What resources and tools have you provided to your constituents—including your corporate partners—that make them feel a sense of ownership of the brand?
- What projects are you currently working on that could be bigger than they are today?
- Are you developing projects and programs that can truly change lives?

"You have a right and a responsibility to lay claim to what touches you and effects change for the future."
—Jodie Foster

* * *

In addition to the things mentioned in this chapter, the wristband campaign also helped all of the staff realize that, as important as it was to think about how the organization distributed its resources and the programs it supported, much of our place in the world was to serve as a beacon of hope and inspiration to the millions of cancer survivors around the world. The brand itself and Lance as a person were what people really needed and craved.

This connection with people was what made the LIVESTRONG wristband campaign and ultimately the organization successful. Relationships with those we serve, with those who could help us, and those who were already fighting for cancer survivors were essential. Looking back there was a common theme throughout each of the partnerships that were most successful—our teams genuinely enjoyed each other and there were strong personal connections that went beyond the business at hand. As a nonprofit organization, we relied on our partners to provide funding and awareness. Rallying an entire community can prove almost impossible with limited resources in the bank. The Foundation needed help and we had to be willing to ask for it. We also needed to prioritize who we asked and maintain a focus on organizations that would be best for the long-term success of the organization. With an eye on the right relationships and a willingness to ask for help, we were ready to build strong connections that would last decades.

Chapter 3

The Right Partnerships

Making the Sum of All Parts Unique

There was one relationship above all else that was responsible for the LIVESTRONG wristband campaign and that was the Foundation's relationship with our point of contact at Nike. His personal connection to cancer, his relationship with Lance, and his access and reputation within Nike provided the Lance Armstrong Foundation (Foundation) with the perfect champion.

The beauty of a company like Nike is that it is filled with brilliant and passionate people. Nike was a true partner in every sense of the word. Unfortunately, partnership is a word that gets used a little too often.

People use it to describe any working relationship between two people or organizations, regardless of the collaboration or resulting impact. The term *partner* loses its meaning when we use it so broadly. The term partner should be reserved for special organizations and relationships that truly create lasting change and are invested in the long-term success of the cause you are representing. Our Nike champion was completely dedicated to the idea of cancer survivorship, the power of the color yellow, and Nike's ability to bottle up the hope and inspiration of Lance and make it widely accessible to millions of people around the world. He spent time getting to know Lance, the cancer community, and our Foundation. He linked that with his intimate knowledge of Nike, its brand and its operations and he leveraged that connection to motivate others internally at Nike to strive for that "simple big idea."

Another indirect benefit of the wristband campaign was that it positioned the Foundation to connect with multiple organizations and develop additional partnerships. The Foundation has been successful in retaining key partnerships because of this ability to select the right partners and to connect with their audience. All of these partners have worked to help LIVESTRONG with continued growth, awareness, and

"You can have anything you want if you want it desperately enough. You must want it with an inner exuberance that erupts through the skin and joins the energy that created the world."

—Sheila Graham

impact and to expand on the amazing corporate out-reach that gained international attention in 2004.

Relying on Others

One of the early steps to developing a true partnership is to ask for help. It seems counter-intuitive to how we've been trained. Usually when we prepare for corporate partnership meetings, we spend all of our time figuring out how to best position our assets and focus on what we have to offer, how they might like to get involved, and why pick us when allocating their company's goodwill. I challenge you to re-frame the conversation as you prepare for your next outreach. Start by discussing how you will ask for help and where they could have a large impact. But, why, you might wonder, ask for help? Because when you ask for help, you are telling that person that you value his or her insights and you feel he or she can make a meaningful impact. You are also recognizing that your case should be about how the help will have a lasting impact and why it is essential for him or her to get involved.

Our missions and our goals are too large to be accomplished alone. It requires the energies, resources, and effort of many. When I start working with an organization and its leaders are unwilling to engage companies in the goals of the organization by asking for help I am always surprised. The reasons why an organization isn't always asking for help can vary. For some it is a sense that no one else cares about the mission and the organization's goals. If this is the case,

"Aim at a high mark and you'll hit it. No, not the first time, nor the second. Maybe not the third. But keep on aiming and keep on shooting for only practice will make you perfect."
—Annie Oakley

they are already defeated before they begin. They will experience a self-fulfilling prophecy.

If you don't believe strongly enough about your cause that you won't ask for help, why would a company want to activate their employees and customers on behalf of your organization? It is important that the people representing the cause be willing to talk at any moment about why someone should get engaged with their organization. Everyone should know the key message about how critical their mission is to those they serve. You are looking for like-minded companies and individuals to help you achieve greatness; in many cases, your mission is life or death. This sense of urgency is important to convey, and being shy about asking for help doesn't help your constituents.

Most nonprofit organizations are not in a position to spend millions of dollars on media buys or able to have a national sales force in every retail outlet in the country. Nonprofits need help in order to efficiently and effectively fulfill their missions. But there are two sides to this, and the other side often goes unstated. Companies need nonprofits, too. Whether in terms of employee engagement, market insights, or simply for fun—companies need and want to help. They spend the majority of their time trying to determine who to help, how best to help, and how their help will benefit the community. The question is: Can we help each other and by doing so will our combined community be better because of it?

Being Selective

In *Monday Morning Choices*[1], David Cotrell recounts a story between two men, Rudy and Jackson. Rudy shared a lesson from his grandmother, "Either walk with the tallest or walk alone." He recommended, "When selecting who you will work with, remember that you should never compromise your values, even if it means going it alone, because it will pay off later." As I stated in Chapter 2, do not diminish the brand or the organization by working with the wrong partners. Partnerships with companies that are not mission-focused or are not good corporate citizens, can definitely hurt your chances for key relationships when the time is right. It is not always easy explaining the decision to pass on an opportunity to companies looking for partnerships, but as long as the decision is values-based, your organization can move past the opportunity with a clean conscience and an eye on the future.

A former advisor once told a group of executive directors that they should say "no" more than they say "yes" when it comes to corporate relationships. One of the most important choices we make is who we associate with, both as individuals and as an

---

[1] *Monday Morning Choices*. David Cotrell. Harper Collins Publishing, New York, NY, 2007.

organization. I recently read that "you are the average of your 10 closest friends." Apply that to cause marketing and corporate partnerships. Continually take inventory of the groups you are associating with and whether or not they will help or hurt your chances for larger relationships in the future. If any given organization examined its 10 closest partnerships, would they be happy with the average? Would they see a need for change?

We take on the characteristics of the people we spend the most time with. Depending on the strength of your current partner roster, this can be good or bad for our mission. One of the first questions asked during the preliminary "getting to know you" meeting is: who have you partnered with in the past? In addition, including a slide in your sponsorship overview about past and current relationships should be seen as a positive. If you question including any of your past sponsors' logos, you should re-examine your decision to have partnered with them in the first place. Every relationship should pass the test of sharing the news of the partnership with the world and feeling proud of the association. If you don't want to communicate the partnership to others, this should be a sign that you probably should have said no to the relationship in the first place.

It is also important to note that this is not a comment on size, geography, industry, or any one specific attribute of a sponsor. Recently, a client was becoming concerned that all of the organization's first round partners were relegated to one region of the United States. The organization's vision was to be a national company and not be impacted by the location of its headquarters. After discussing the situation, I advised the organization not to focus on the location of the partners, but rather focus on the industries they represented, their connection to larger national companies, and the ability to use the insights gained from their partnership for future modeling. It is always good to be selective, but be sure that your filter is supporting your vision and that you aren't just asking standard questions—customization is key.

Pinpointing Where Real Engagement Happens

As a sales person for an event company, I quickly realized that companies don't buy products and services—people do. On paper, the relationship is between two organizations. But, the real engagement happens between two people. The wristband campaign would not have been possible without our Nike champion's intimate knowledge of Lance and the Foundation.

> *"While we are influenced by circumstance, we, too, can have an influence."*
> —Jonas Salk

Provide every opportunity for your partners and prospects to engage with your team, your constituents, and your community. They may see something that you missed and will bring it to your attention. They may find inspiration where you least expect it.

While representing the Autism Society of America, we had an opportunity to engage a new corporate partner, Pump It Up. Both organizations wanted to get involved and there was a clear alignment of audiences. The question became how to make the concept meaningful, mission related, and impactful. After spending time with families affected by autism, there was a revelation. The physical therapists that worked with the children used inflatable jumpers like the ones at Pump It Up during therapy. The goal was then to create an event that would utilize the Pump It Up locations to bring both affected and non-affected families together in a fun and safe environment. Bounce for autism happened because the nonprofit engaged everyone in the process, including vendors, families, and the prospective partner. The event launched and was a success for both partners. Pump It Up franchisees met people in their communities that wanted to use the facilities on a regular year-round basis. Families were educated about autism and additional funds were raised for the cause.

Make the process of engagement interesting for everyone. This includes those representatives from the partner or partner prospect. And don't limit yourself to your immediate point of contact. Engage board members, administrative assistants, team members, and customers—everyone willing to invest time in you and your cause. During our interview for the writing of this book, Bianca provided a good reminder that your most likely candidate for a meaningful partner is probably right in your own backyard. Look internally at existing supporters and really engage them.

Your organization's next wristband campaign is probably right in front of you. Those that have already demonstrated a willingness to help will be the most receptive to ideas of growth. Progress is more likely and they will be eager to get on board in an impactful way.

This is also a reminder about your time and how you choose to spend it. When you spend time with an individual or an organization, you are making an investment of your time—a limited and precious resource. Some partners will lift you up and allow you to achieve things beyond your wildest imagination, but others can drain you and prevent you from achieving your goals. Including this core, committed group in your prospect list is very important. When you assess the list and prioritize, be sure to think about how you spend your time and where it is most valuable.

Learning from Conflicts

As with any relationship, conflict will arise. Be prepared and have a clear plan of action to address the issues. There were several times when items from sponsors would not arrive in time for Ride Weekend. Each of these moments of adversity presented an opportunity to build more rapport with the various partners. By working through the issues side by side the relationships were strengthened because of it. Then, when larger issues would arise on a specific cause-marketing campaign, we had an already established strong working relationship to lean on. We quickly and efficiently addressed the problems at hand without worrying about jeopardizing the larger partnership.

"I believe that you can get everything in life you want if you will help enough other people get what they want."
—Zig Ziglar

During the campaign and during challenging operational issues, each partner showed grace and patience to one another. We grew together and the relationship has continued to grow because of that trust and knowledge that everyone is coming from a good place. You will know you are on the right track when you feel a sense of "we're in this together."

Building Strong Connections

Truly meaningful partnerships, as mentioned earlier, don't happen overnight. You have to be committed to building strong connections. If you are new to an organization or trying to jump-start growth in an existing company or charity, there are an unlimited number of ways to cultivate and steward partners. My first few weeks at the Foundation in 2000 were spent making as many connections as possible.

When I arrived at the Foundation on my first day of work I was given an office in the very back of the little yellow house where our offices were located. In the office was a large metal filing cabinet. I remember opening the first drawer and pulling out the first manila folder. Inside was a scrap of paper that had the name Bobby written on it and a phone number. I immediately picked up the phone and dialed Bobby. We talked for a few minutes and I learned that he had supplied the tents to the Ride for the Roses event. He was able to provide me with inventory lists, site layout drawings, and most importantly, ideas to improve the event. That was the first call. That day, I made myself a promise that I would talk either in person or by phone to every one of the people whose name was contained in the filing cabinet. The calls started with a Ride for the Roses equipment company, and included people like Scott MacEachern from Nike. Each call was the start of a relationship between myself and someone motivated by Lance and the Foundation's mission.

If you don't have file folders filled with contacts or access to an established database—create one! Join as many groups as possible. Learn from your peers. Subscribe to journals, magazines, and newsletters. Call the people you read about in articles. They will take your calls. I have never been turned down for a 15-minute phone conversation. People have an interest in helping, so be sure to give them a chance.

> *"All things being equal, people want to do business with their friends."*
> —Jeffrey Gitomer

A strong connection can start anywhere and at any time. I have such fond memories of the partners of the Lance Armstrong Foundation. Each one has their own story of how it got started. I consider each a friend and always enjoyed our conversations. I looked forward to talking with them. We shared our excitement about the possibilities for the organization and our partnership. I have been fortunate to continue my relationships with many of these individuals long after I departed the Foundation and I am encouraged to see so many of them still involved on a daily basis with the Foundation. I believe the relationships have lasted because people felt a sense of ownership and belonging.

People want to feel a sense of belonging and it is important for you to introduce and foster relationships across partners. Host partner summits, exchange contact information, and make e-introductions or invite everyone to events throughout the year and dedicate networking time to this very important audience segment.

Provide opportunities to connect. You are the glue that binds the partners together. It is your job to help them connect the dots that will provide the biggest impact for your organization. Steward this group as you would your event participants, major donors, or board members. It is likely that you have the stewardship tools and systems in place but haven't applied them to your partnership efforts. Determining the tactics is a part of the process, but step one is making the commitment to connect.

Being Genuine by Showing Your True Self

There is often a lot of pressure when you are connecting with others. As an executive of a non-profit or a representative of a company, we feel the pressure to paint the organization in the best possible light. We quickly downplay the things about the organization that need fixing or adjustment. However, real progress is made when we show our true selves—good and bad.

After being diagnosed, Lance feared calling his sponsors. As a professional cyclist, he did not have insurance. He could not afford to lose his sponsors because of the diagnosis. He faced his fears and made the calls. The first sponsor he called was Scott from Nike. Lance told Scott about the cancer and his concerns about no longer being a Nike athlete. Scott said, "We'll take care of you." And they did.

Scott and Nike focused on the needs of their athlete and the already-established relationship. They were interested in helping him get the help he needed. From this experience you can see that something that was once feared as a weakness by Lance later become one of his greatest accomplishments after he overcame the odds and went on to win the Tour de France a record-breaking seven times.

If we are honest about who we are currently and where we are headed, we can appreciate each other more. Then, and only then, can we find ways to help that truly make a difference. Does this mean you should tell your partner that there are five members of your staff that are not working up to your organization's standards or that your technology platform is in disarray and needs a complete overhaul? No. It simply means that you should not go into these conversations trying to be someone or something you are not.

You should be clear about what stage of maturity your organization is in and clearly articulate where you hope to be. You should be able to provide an overview of the organization's strengths and assets as well as point out those things that might interfere with your success. Ask for advice and help to remove them as roadblocks. I once received a piece of artwork that said, "He loved her for *almost* everything she was, so she decided to let him stay a while." Apply this to your corporate relationships. The same can be applied to your partnerships. You are not going to see eye to eye on every matter. You may not like that your partner has some areas in need of improvement. However, these are opportunities for you to build on and positively impact. Your partnerships should be long term, and with that comes a level of comfort and acceptance for the whole, not just the parts that benefit you or your organization.

Engaging and Equipping Champions

While you typically are focused on creating a strong connection within the partner organization, remember than many cause-marketing and corporate-partnership decisions are made by committee, or at a minimum are influenced by a committee recommendation. This is why your internal champion at the partnering organization is critical, but can't be your only point of contact.

While you are working to enlarge the circle of influence within the partner organization, you must dedicate the resources and time to your primary champion. The champion should be intimately knowledgeable about the goals of the partnership. He or she should be able to convey them effectively within the respective organizations. The goal is to elevate your relationship with the champion to the role of an advisor and trusted ally. Charles Schultz, creator of the famous Peanuts characters, once said:

"While people may or may not long remember who won what award, contest, or prize or set which world record—they will always remember someone who has listened to them, appreciated, or helped them in solving a problem or overcoming an obstacle."

The two of you are working together to affect change. As the person responsible for partnerships, spend time thinking about what would help your ally move ahead in their organization. Provide those resources and tools. This can be everything from typing their quarterly report about your organization so they have a draft to start from to helping them craft internal emails or dashboard reports. Being fully invested in both the company's success and the success of the individual will benefit your organization in the short and long term. Never hesitate to pick up the phone instead of sending an email and always apply the Golden Rule when dealing with partners. "Do unto others as you would have them do unto you."

> *"This isn't personal, it's just biz." is the dumbest quote I have heard. All business is very personal at every level.*
> —Robert Dickie III

Welcoming Variety

Partnerships of all shapes and sizes are necessary to keep things moving forward. Nike was the most visible relationship that we had and we experienced a tremendous amount of exposure through them. But, there were other Foundation partners that had a lasting impact as well. Many of these relationships evolved over time similar to the partnership with Nike.

When reviewing your current list of partners, do not miss an opportunity to expand or revise your relationship. Whether you transition from a marketing partner to a content-creator or from an event sponsorship to a marketing relationship, each relationship should be re-evaluated regularly. Be sure you know what new products and services your partners are trying to reach. Communicate the strengths and areas of development for your organization effectively so you can continually brainstorm on ways to work together and make a positive impact on the communities you care about. Once you have done this successfully a few times, you will be able to use the model as a template for future organizations becoming actively involved with your programs and the lifecycle of a partner can be identified.

Every partnership, large or small, can impact the bottom line of both organizations and can provide a net benefit. As partners, it is your task to uncover those opportunities that require minimal effort but that can have tremendous positive outcomes. This can only occur when two partners know each other well and share openly in a variety of forums.

The Science of Selection

Determining whether or not to engage with a specific organization can sometimes feel very subjective. Depending on the whims of the person responsible for the partnership, a prospective partner may or may not be pursued. This process should be more objective. It should align with the strategy, vision, and mission of the organization. To transform our process from a subjective process to an objective one, we implemented a partnership and brand filter.

The filter started with brand questions at the top. It asked the standard questions such as, "Do our missions match up?" We also asked questions specifically about the Foundation's brand attributes. Then we would get more specific about whether the partnership would impact our fundraising efforts, advocacy, and programs or propel the movement forward in general through marketing and advertising support. Another challenge is the need to understand a potential partner's motivation for involvement with the organization. Always ask why an organization wants to get involved with your organization and the cause. If you are ever in a situation where you can't easily explain why a company would be interested in your organization, pause and hit the reset button. Knowing and understanding each other's motivation for the relationship is a must and is not a step that can be skipped.

If "no" was answered to any of the questions, the champion for that partner was asked to re-examine the opportunity and provide a clear case for support. After several rounds of revisions and input from individuals both inside and outside the organization, we began using the tool as a way to gauge the potential for every new partner. It really served as a decision tree and it was something that could be modified for other departments within the organization. Through the process, we identified groups that were aligned but were not being maximized. We also had a few relationships that we needed to create an exit strategy for. These were not easy conversations to have and the transitions didn't happen overnight. We used the filter as a tool and it gave us the confidence we needed to take difficult actions that were in the best interest of the Foundation. After the filter was developed, it wasn't restricted to new partner evaluation. Our first step was to allocate time to examining our current partners to determine if we should make retention of that partner a priority. While not always a perfect system, it did provide everyone with a tool and it forced people to ask the hard questions and truly think through partnership engagement.

Leveraging Organizational Structure and Interactions

Companies should also be evaluating potential charity partners with a filter that aligns their core values, strategic priorities, mission, and vision. One aspect of the Foundation that I feel was of interest to Nike when they did their own internal assessment about the organization was that we were centrally managed. We had a grassroots network of people and we did not have the additional layers of decision from chapters. I am currently working with a national organization with chapters and regional leadership offices. I am participating as a member of their corporate initiatives task force. The four committees within the task force are charged with creating a prospect list, defining policies and guidelines, development of marketing collateral, and partner opportunities. The task force has been created with a combination of national, regional, and local team members and each brings a unique set of experiences and challenges to the conversation.

When dealing with an organization that not only has a national brand, but also includes local or regional chapters there are additional issues and opportunities. These need to be considered when trying to build a campaign such as the LIVESTRONG wristband campaign. In some ways, it would have been great to have hundreds of chapters to help distribute and promote the wristbands. On the other hand, I can also see the difficulty in moving a large ship quickly. Being a nimble organization that could direct activities quickly from a central location was attractive to Nike, but these same things might not be important to another partner. Be sure your organizational structure is an asset to your partner and determine how to leverage it.

> *"No road is long with good company."*
> —Turkish Proverb

The culture of the Lance Armstrong Foundation and Nike helped to create a wonderful working environment and close working relationship with a strong core of people. Nike put their best people on launching the campaign. They spent hours with us talking about branding, logistics, employee involvement, and more. They leveraged every asset at their disposal to bring attention to the wristband. They reached out to Nike athletes, worked with Niketown stores to give us space in stores, and reached out to their resellers for support. We were able to leverage their amazing creative team to develop the web site, the commercials for radio and TV, and our print campaign. At times, it felt surreal to have been blessed with such gifts and we thought about pinching ourselves. But then, we would be reminded why everyone was rallying. A Nike employee would open up about his or her cancer connection and we would be reminded that everyone has been impacted by this disease. Everyone felt empowered to be working on the campaign. Our mission was a shared one and when that happens there are no resources off limits.

We spent many long hours together and there was always tons of laughter to go along with the serious conversations. We appreciated each other's organizational cultures and ways of doing business. The team at the Foundation learned so much from Nike and I truly believe that continues to positively influence the success of LIVESTRONG today. Likewise, I would like to think that the experience of dealing with our team opened Nike's eyes to the potential of full-investment in a cause and the assets that a charity can bring to the table.

Many companies choose to maintain event sponsorships and in-kind support of a select group of designated charities. Nike and companies like it struggle with how they would ever choose between all the worthy organizations, including all of the causes of other athletes or key team members. But, after the campaign, Scott admitted that sometimes the cause chooses you. Since the campaign, Nike continues to interact positively and on a large scale with their customers and the causes they care about. They impact millions of people a year and I am glad that the Lance Armstrong Foundation was a part of their corporate social responsibility history. My hope is that by working with our team, they were able to see how they could better serve nonprofits and how to better work together for shared passions.

Fostering Evolution

It is important to note that the relationship with Nike continued to evolve since those early days in 2000. When you are working on a partnership or campaign, be sure to think strategically about what this relationship may look like in six months, a year, or five years. Evolution is inevitable and the partnership will evolve with or without your helping hand. You want to work to keep the conversation relevant for each of you at various stages of your organization. A few helpful questions to ask include:

- How much do you know about your key partners?
- Are they looking to enter new markets?
- Are they expanding or reducing their workforces?
- What might their biggest challenges or opportunities be down the road?
- How can you help or influence those things?

Luckily, the dialogue between Nike and the Foundation continued long past the wristband campaign. With an open dialogue, the partners can make adjustments and the relationship will continue to be mutually beneficial. Expansions of the Nike and LIVESTRONG partnership included the addition of running events to the Ride Weekend, now the LIVESTRONG Challenge and the growth of Team LIVESTRONG.

The wristband campaign communicates to companies that "Doing the right thing can be good for the bottom line."

> "In everyone's life, at some time, our inner fire goes out. It is then burst into flame by an encounter with another human being. We should all be thankful for those people who rekindle the inner spirit."
>
> —Albert Schweitzer

Try to have a few tricks up your sleeves at all times that will provide new ideas for engagement with your organization or your audience. Options include introductions to new audience segments, program interactions, committee or board involvement—the options are unlimited. The key is being strategic about the path you would like them to follow and helping to facilitate that growth. You must also be adaptable to changes in the path but think through what the partnership will look like in two years or 10 years. How are you working them toward that goal? What will they need to know in order to make those kinds of commitments to your organization? Make that happen.

*   *   *

Truly great partners will not only deliver great results but they will provide unprecedented access to their internal workings. Be prepared to learn from your partners and vendors regarding planning techniques, industry insights, and more. The ability to carry those resources over into our planning at the Foundation set us up for success not only for this campaign but for all other planning in the future.

The beauty of the wristband campaign is that the partnership between Nike and the Foundation captured the intangible—it focused on the outcome and the experience instead of the product or service. It gave survivors the ability to connect to one another. We did not focus on the band itself as the end deliverable. The end result was a visible and connected cancer survivorship community. The band was the mechanism or vehicle—a means to an end. The president of Anthropologie, Glen Shenk, once said, "Our focus is on always doing what's right for a specific customer we know every well. Our customers are our friends, and what we do is never, ever, ever about selling to them."

Always take time to learn from others especially your partners. Read about other success stories, study other industries, and look for models that might apply to your situation or help you achieve your goals. The Lance Armstrong Foundation sought to bring together experts with varied backgrounds to best position the organization for success. As the leadership team, we were constantly being exposed to individuals and organizations that were experts in various topics and we took something away from every conversation and exchange and those pieces added up to LIVESTRONG. Once the campaign was under way, it was even more important to seek the best advice and smartly build what would become our merchandise and cause-marketing team. Along the way, each person also made a commitment to providing this type of leadership and knowledge share to others while continuing to strive for excellence. In order to truly grow you have to expose yourself to experts and be willing to learn and evolve from those experiences.

Chapter 4

Pinpointing Experts and Utilizing Their Strengths

Everyone is an expert in something. For some, it's teaching. For others, it can be driving. In the case of Nike and the Lance Armstrong Foundation (Foundation), it was marketing and understanding the cancer community and its needs. Nike came to the table in 2004 with an appreciation that the Foundation was best positioned to distribute $6 million in funding for the cancer community. They entrusted us to leverage those

"I not only use all the brains I have, but all I can borrow."

—Woodrow Wilson

funds to ensure they would have the best possible impact. Likewise, the Foundation acknowledged that Nike was the expert in branding and marketing and getting consumers to "Just Do It." By partnering together we were able to leverage each other's strengths and assets.

Leveraging Your Partners

I have relayed the phrase "know thyself" in this book, and, in the case of Nike and the Foundation, it has been applied to the organizations, the teams, the audiences, and more. In the case of Nike, they definitely "know thyself." And they are willing to use this knowledge of their strengths to benefit the greater good. The following is an excerpt from the presentation from Scott at Nike to the Foundation:

> ". . . starting in May 2004, we'll spread the gospel of Lance Armstrong by showing the impact that Lance has on people everywhere, inviting people to join Lance on his journey for his sixth Tour and celebrating the magnitude of his sixth victory. How? By doing what we do best: An epic spot about Lance in combination with a simple impactful BIG idea. When combining these two elements we align all of our marketing power to make sure people truly know what's about to happen and at the same time give people an opportunity to become emotionally and personally connected."

Preparing the Foundation for the impending success and increased awareness was not an easy task. We relied heavily on our board members, vendors, partners, mentors, and other industry leaders. Each member of the Foundation team spoke regularly with external peers and sought knowledge about a variety of topics. Whether it was talking with the team at the fulfillment house about shipping and customer service questions, or calling our friends from the cancer community for insights and feedback on potential charity partnerships, or calling on cyclists for events, we were always looking for experts to talk to and learn from.

The phrase "let me run something by you" was something we said often. People are happy to be considered experts on a given topic and are usually very agreeable to helping. You must be respectful of their time and understand any boundaries that should be considered, but for the most part if you ask, they will help. Along with acknowledging any boundaries, you should be clear about where you are in the planning stages. This includes telling them how you intend to use the information, other points of view you are considering, and, if there is a decision to be made, when you plan to make it. And be sure to tell them if you are just in the idea-formation stages. Sometimes what you are going to do with these key insights is still undetermined, but you can sense value in just having the conversation and expanding your knowledge base.

The receptiveness at the Foundation to do things differently allowed the organization to have its house in order which positioned us for optimal success at the time of the wristband launch. Being an expert is sometimes just a matter of asking the right questions and forcing the team to think through the possibilities and the potential scenarios. Doing this can provide a variety of models to reference when the time comes. By pre-examining those models, you can better prepare your organization for new opportunities that present themselves. This all becomes easier if you make an effort to surround yourself with smart people. Remember, you are the average of your 10 closest friends.

> *"There's a way to do it better—find it."*
> —Thomas Edison

Gaining Expertise in Merchandise

The launch of the wristband campaign created the need for a variety of new expertise. Some of these needs were temporary, while others would become a part of the organization as long as wristbands were being sold. The first area that we identified was merchandise and inventory management. With the success of the wristband campaign it was obvious that we needed to identify some experts in the world of merchandise. Luckily, Emy Settle and Missy Douthit became involved and helped bring their knowledge of the industry to the campaign. Prior to joining the team at the Foundation, Missy Douthit was a volunteer. She had spent the past 15 years working in merchandise management and retail buying and inventory management. Missy quickly began implementing best practices from her retail experience that made a huge difference in our behind-the-scenes operations. She was able to explain the reasoning behind requests from resellers that we weren't familiar with. She worked with our accounting team to establish proper tracking and measurement tools. She also helped us know when we needed to push back with Nike on a given merchandise topic and what was acceptable from our vendors for fulfillment, packaging, and more. After recognizing her ability to help the Foundation implement processes and operations, and realizing that the wristband was going to have an on-going influence on the organization, Missy became the director of merchandise within the Development Department.

Prior to the wristband campaign, the revenue structure for the Foundation was fairly traditional with events, sponsorships, direct marketing, and major giving serving as the primary revenue sources. We had a proven track record for diversifying our revenue streams and had gone from event and unsolicited white mail in 1999 to a wide range of donor engagement options. We did learn that every new revenue opportunity presents new challenges including things like unrelated business income tax issues, fulfillment challenges, and implementation of best practices. In order to make sure the best possible path is taken, reach out to other vendors, contractors, and partners. Each can help your organization address a specific challenge and ensure that the organization remains in good standing with your constituents.

Be sure to take full advantage of hiring expertise on contract when it is deemed necessary but you are unsure of the longevity of a specific program or initiative. Every organization should be resistant to adding headcount because typically the needs of the organization will be very different one year into a campaign or after the campaign starts to flatten out. It is probable that at every turn there will be a decision to be made about creating an internal position to manage a project or hire someone temporarily under contract. At the Foundation, we constantly evaluated the internal expertise level on a given topic and the team's bandwidth. Be sure to acknowledge when it is appropriate to look outside the organization. Outsourcing and the utilization of contract workers with short-term renewable contracts can allow your organization to stay flexible and make adjustments at key milestones as new information becomes available. When talking about the wristband campaign and the use of outsourcing, one of the members of the campaign team stressed the importance of managing those vendors from within. It is not always as turn-key as you would hope and having the appropriate checks and balances is essential. It is not as simple as handing over the project and being able to walk away. There is still a management of the contractor or vendor that needs to happen. Having systems in place at the time of signing contracts can be very helpful for both parties. These checkpoints allowed us to all work together when a new or never seen before problem came up. Just as Nike and the Foundation were gracious and patient, the Foundation worked with our vendors to make our way together through this uncharted territory. Everyone was working as hard as they possibly could and we would not have been successful motivating with fear. We felt positive

"Be easy on yourself and everyone else. We are all works in progress."
—David Cottrell

motivation and an understanding of how their part related to the entire campaign was more inspiring and more in line with how the Foundation did business.

When creating a program like the wristband campaign, it was imperative that we identified each partner's strengths and captured them in the organizational structure of the project. The Foundation provided a certain skill set but was lacking in other skill sets such as manufacturing. It was important to determine early on who would be handling various tasks. We went so far as to create an organizational chart that merged the two campaign teams together and formed one super-organization. We took the best from both organizations to set us up for the greatest chance of success. We also identified places within the organizational structure of the campaign team where team members would need to work together to get things done. This included marketing, media relations, event integration, and more. Next time you are building a cause-marketing campaign, think about it like you would if you were starting a new business. Along with creating the financial analysis, look at whether or not you have all the bases covered to really launch the company or effort. You can see gaps and work together to fill those or, at a minimum, identify the resources before you actually need them so it doesn't slow down the process.

While you are creating this overview of the campaign team structure, think about which positions or segments of the campaign you would like to learn more about. Making sure that learning is built into the project can help prolong the positive impact of the effort. As an example, understanding more of the technology options considered for the back end of the campaign allowed the development team to learn about other ways to engage donors outside of the wristband. Or, working hand-in-hand with the Nike media relations team exposed us to new ways to work with the media and how we might have better success if we implemented a few new rules and ideas. Executing the campaign well was important and we were focused on setting ourselves up for the greatest possible chance for success. But, it turned out to be equally important for us to shadow and learn from one another because the opportunity to learn from experts during execution is rare and it is has a much longer impact for the organization and the individuals involved.

Leveraging Your Leadership

When I think about the number of people that influenced the success of the Foundation it is overwhelming. We truly could not have done it without them. The Foundation was filled with amazing people that, even if they were alone, would be game-changers for an organization. Here we were talking about putting all of those powerhouses into one room and seeing where we could go. But you cannot sit back and wait for these types of individuals to reach out to you and ask how they can help. You need to think through their involvement and how you are going to leverage their influence and expertise. Just as with major giving strategies, there is a stewardship path you help facilitate and the same should be done for your leadership's involvement in a cause-marketing campaign. How you will get them invested in the idea, what networks they can influence to encourage support, and possibly even bringing partners to the table are all things to consider. The first step is understanding who those leaders are within your organization.

Who are your experts and leaders? I was fortunate to have someone like Mike Sherwin, a Foundation board member, available for guidance and mentoring. I still have the list of questions we created together after we first learned of the wristband campaign concept. Who do you call when you have a question you can't answer or an idea you need to talk through? Fostering those relationships can be the most important thing you do, not only for the organization you represent but for you personally.

There is no way that one person can possibly keep up with every detail, new technology, or industry factoid. The really powerful people know how to rally a team of experts to move their projects and missions forward. Lance did this when he started the Foundation. The LIVESTRONG staff does it today by engaging with chief executive officers (CEOs) of Fortune 500 companies and attending conferences and workshops and by making continuing education and the pursuit of information a priority for its leadership.

If the organization is going to serve as a catalyst for change, it must first know what is going on, including trends within and outside of its direct influence. From hosting the Global Summit to the LIVESTRONG Assembly, the Foundation continues to leverage the expertise of many.

Lance knew when he started the Foundation that he would need to surround himself with thought leaders and company builders. He went out and recruited leadership from the venture capital community and business entrepreneurs. He identified those individuals early in their careers with the experience and potential for greatness that could be harnessed for his cause. He fully leveraged experts.

And leveraging your leadership does not mean you are only involving them in big-picture conversations or long-term-strategy conversations. Think about all of the various stages they can plug into and impact. This could simply mean a phone call or facilitating an introduction to interacting with the CEO of a partner prospect's company to talk peer to peer about the opportunity. There have been times in my career where I have had to admit that I might not be the best person for the job. The difference is not forcing it or giving up and walking away. It is first to have that revelation and then to identify the person who can create the path of least resistance for the prospect. Sometimes that was finding someone in the office that was a huge fan of a given product and bringing them along to strategy sessions and partner pitches. Other times, it was knowing where there might be a connection between two personalities and leveraging that to establish rapport with a partner. Know your assets, including those of your leadership, and be sure to identify ways for them to engage. They will be eager to help—that is why they signed on in the first place either to the staff, the board, advisory committees, or more. Everyone wants to feel useful, so be sure to think about how they can help and it will be a win-win for everyone involved.

Combining the Right People

As an event manager early in my career to president of my own consulting company, I am constantly trying to determine the right people for the job. Earlier we discussed getting to know people, and now it is time to put the pieces of the puzzle together. And someone might be right at one given point in time but the needs of the group may change and a new set of skills is required. During the interview for the book, Randall Macon and I spoke about the need to think about recruitment for the Foundation in those early years of the campaign. We knew the organization would be growing, but our hiring needs changed dramatically as our infrastructure, programs, and development efforts continued to evolve.

I often refer to *Good to Great*[1] and Jim Collins' concept of finding the right people to invite on the bus. Some of the problems we were encountering had not been dealt with before, so there was not a perfect candidate for the task at hand. It required an ability to focus on the desired skill sets instead of looking for direct experience. Randall himself is an example of this. His background in design wouldn't necessarily translate to the creation of an online resource for cancer survivors or a director of innovation, but he

[1] *Good to Great*. Jim Collins. New York, NY, Harper Collins Publishers, 2001.

was perfect for the job. Doug Ulman is another example of finding an expert. As a young cancer survivor, Doug did not have decades of work experience, but his vision matched where Lance and the board saw the Foundation in the future. Doug was an expert in knowing the cancer community and continues to be one of the most networked and knowledgeable CEOs I have ever met.

Scott was our expert for all things Nike. He helped us navigate the internal workings of the company and was the right person for the job. He guided us through countless presentations and outreach efforts and also trained us along the way on dealing with their retailers, suppliers, and other key partners. If you have the opportunity to be part of a campaign like the wristband campaign, I encourage you to be a sponge. Soak up every bit of knowledge and expertise made available to you. The LIVESTRONG campaign had a lasting impact on me personally and professionally and I am grateful for those opportunities to exchange ideas with some amazing individuals. I am glad I had a seat on the bus.

"Every winner has scars."
—Herbert Casson

There will be people along the journey that will be invited on the bus who quickly realized they are not a fit long term. This is not always a bad thing but rather an opportunity for those who are already on the team and engaged to see firsthand what makes them unique as a group. Just as you should be filtering potential partners through your mission and values, you should also be determining who gets on the bus by learning if there will be a cultural fit with the organization, how they will interact with the team, and what you think they will contribute to the organization that is beyond what you currently are capable of.

Also, while it is always ideal to have experts focused on every aspect of a campaign or operation, the likelihood of that happening in most organizations is pretty small. The majority of people find themselves in a position of increased demands on their time, an increased realm of responsibility, and a need to innovate and do more with less. There is a need to do things more efficiently and effective every step of the way.

I have realized that truly successful people are able to specialize when needed and never shy away from doing something new or unexpected. It is never readily apparent what one will learn from doing something in a different department or how exposure to another company's culture may positively impact your own outlook on your organization. Being a jack of all trades is the norm and not the exception. I hear people often talk about this Shangri-la where everyone gets to focus 110 percent of their energy on one task, but have never actually seen or experienced it first-hand. Honestly, I am not sure I would ever be content with that type of organization or opportunity. It doesn't leave much room for the possibilities.

Documenting Your Journey

Reflecting back on the campaign experience, I want to remind you to document and make notes about the lessons learned in various campaigns you are involved with. Having a journal or similar documents to draw from and match up similar experiences will position you as an expert for others in some form or fashion in the future. You will wish you had written down those things you would do differently and the ideas or comments you wish you could share with the world.

One idea is to set aside 15 minutes at the beginning of each day for writing. The topic can vary and you may later begin to see clear topic headings, but the point is really just to make writing a habit. There could be so much learned from a cause-marketing professional creating a blog to track the creation of a cause-marketing campaign from start to finish. I have seen similar article series or blogs on companies being acquired or event-concept generation, but have not seen a resource where someone in our profession was sharing the entire lifecycle of the process and the outcomes.

If writing a blog or journaling seems out of character for you, there are several other tools to help facilitate this today that weren't as prevalent in 2004. I like to think that if Twitter or Facebook were being used more during the launch of our campaign, our team would have captured those "a-ha" moments and lessons learned in real time. Instead, because it was before the advent of the popular "140 characters or less" lifestyle we now live in, I find myself poring over old composition notebooks, photographs, phone logs, and memorabilia to uncover those hidden gems and most meaningful lessons from the LIVESTRONG campaign. The point of all of this is to share your expertise and not let that knowledge stay hidden. Help others.

Finding and Giving Feedback, and Knowing What to Filter

Another admirable trait about Nike is their humility. The employees were always willing to ask questions and never hesitated to ask why. They used every opportunity to learn something new and surrounded themselves with experts both internally and externally. One of the things I learned from the team at Nike was to filter all advice. Just because a model works for one organization or campaign does not necessarily mean it is the right solution for your problem or opportunity. Read, investigate, learn, listen, and discuss, but always use this information as data-points for building your own solution. Don't take any one piece of advice or recommendation as the only answer. Rarely is there a one-size-fits-all approach to anything. Your job isn't to find the right answer. It is to create the right answer based on the information you have available as it applies to your specific situation.

> *"What's the best way to climb a mountain on a bike, given my gifts?"*
>
> —Lance Armstrong

There were many times that I had a revelation during a conversation or would feel like I had all the answers only to learn after a brief encounter with someone else that I needed to rethink the whole situation. Each of these decision milestones and experiences provided me with an inventory to apply to various opportunities or problems needing solutions. While my experience has been great, I always try to remember the power of saying "I don't know" or admitting that I might not be the best possible person to answer the question. Every time you provide an expert opinion on something that you truly have no expertise on, you reduce the amount of trust and respect your peers and colleagues have for you. A willingness to find the right answer is much more impressive and allows both you and the person you are helping to learn together.

In addition to remembering when to say "I don't know," it is equally important to remember that unsolicited advice or stating that you are the expert on a given topic is never welcomed or appreciated. This is true when talking with your partners, your peers, and anyone in general. If someone feels like you have the expertise or knowledge to positively impact their work, they will ask for your opinion when and if they want it.

"If people knew how hard I worked to get my mastery, it wouldn't seem so wonderful at all."
—Michelangelo

Further, asking for advice requires a willingness to talk about your problems, discuss everything, and create a relationship of acceptance and comfort to share positive and negative feelings. My family received an amazing book called *Season of Life*[2]. While the text is focused on raising boys into men, the main lesson is to live your life for others. This lesson is universal. I have found that most people in our industry live by this motto. They are usually ready and willing to share their insights and lessons. You just have to ask. But be aware that you might not always like what you hear. Along with expert advice can come criticism. If you

[2] *Season of Life.*

are really open to the feedback, it can lead to trans-formational improvements. When Jeff Garvey was serving as Executive Director, he implemented a simple but powerful annual-review template. It was on one page and it had two sections: Accomplishments and Needs Improvement. Each section contained three bullet points. I don't remember what was under Accomplishments, but I remember exactly what was listed in the second section. I learned more from that feedback than the celebration of work well done.

Continuously strive to learn from others and invest in your own education. This can include reading, attending conferences and seminars, serving as a mentor, or simply looking for new opportunities to expand your current frame of reference. These efforts can dramatically impact your thinking. Two instances I can recall that have influenced me recently include:

1. A Board Chairman who was an expert in early American history related fascinating stories about George Washington's patience and leadership style to the struggles of a national organization and its varied chapter leadership; and,
2. Joe Aragona, a board member at the Foundation and long-time advisor, applied his expertise in building companies as a venture capitalist to help grow the Foundation. He demanded the highest quality of every organization endeavor.

Be sure you are exposing yourself to constant learning and try to spend time thinking about some of the highlights from those experiences and interactions.

*   *   *

Experts will shape and influence you and the future of your organization, so choose wisely and do not leave this to chance. Be strategic and thoughtful and identify key points in your growth where experts can make a positive difference. You will know you are talking to someone who can help the future of your organization when they help you focus on key drivers and filter through the clutter and noise. You can also work with your advisors and experts to provide resources and tools to help you chart your course for the future.

Looking back at the history of the organization and reviewing key milestones can be helpful, but taking the time to talk with peers and your constituents about the roadmap for the future will be time better spent. Excellence requires a focus on constant improvement and does not allow you to wait for future success to come because of past victories. You have to keep fighting and finding those opportunities for greatness.

Chapter 5

The Role of Strategic Planning in Your Mission's Success

At any given point in time, the average non-profit executive is trying to manage a two-page to-do list, spend all day in meetings, filter and direct an exorbitant number of opportunities and projects, and work to maintain countless relationships. It is easy to get caught up in the details of the job and lose sight of the big picture. The executive leadership of the organization can quickly become consumed with tasks related to small projects or upcoming deadlines. This is why it is important to recognize opportune moments throughout the year when visualizing and discussing the future is the priority. These moments include project kick-off meetings, board meetings, advisory group sessions, and scheduling one-on-one conversations with people who you know will force you to think differently and reexamine your current way of operating.

Organizations will go for months focused on the day-to-day operations. An entire quarter will pass before you hear a mention of those ambitious long-term goals you set last year. Typically everyone will stop and start asking questions again only when something is breaking or not going as planned instead of assessing the progress along the way and looking for constant improvement. This ongoing assessment and examination provides for those small tweaks and changes that can make a huge difference. It can also identify red flags and barriers to success earlier and remedy the situations before they permeate other parts of the organization.

Taking time to plan and ask the right questions while gaining insights from others and leveraging every opportunity to its fullest does not come naturally. You must be committed to making it a priority. For some this means establishing quarterly reviews or setting reminders on a calendar. To others it is writing reminders that get posted on the wall or above the door. While the task of strategic planning can be daunting, it can relieve the anxiety and fear of the unknown. Having the ability to talk through various scenarios in a calm and structured environment is a gift that should be treasured. There will come a time for every organization when a sense of urgency and need for immediate action prohibits long-term assessment. This is when pulling from those earlier planning and assessment sessions will be most valuable. Having the ability to go into those situations with confidence and a sense of knowledge can set the tone for both your team internally and also give your partners and the larger community a feeling of confidence in your ability to achieve results.

Making Time to Plan

Remind yourself constantly about the need to plan. This can be a perfect place for outside consultation. Establish a relationship that allows someone who is not involved in the daily activities of your organization to touch base occasionally with you. They will have the ability to check in periodically and help you assess the organization from a higher level. This can be a function of the board, a request you make of a corporate partner, or a mutual agreement with a peer. These planning sessions can be as complex or simple as you want them to be. Making an impact on your future and the future of your organization does not require thousands of whiteboard sessions or five rounds of revisions on a strategic map.

Do not put this type of planning off because you imagine a huge project, but rather look for moments already available to you where you can elevate the conversation. Many of my current clients have weekly development team meetings that become reporting sessions on last week's accomplishments or the upcoming week's to-do list. Use one meeting a month to talk about planning. Start by discussing your planning process and assessing its efficacy and relevance. Then make a list of all of the planning opportunities for the team and prioritize them. Use the next month to test the new process. Make adjustments and move on to the rest of the list. Some planning can be done in minutes and other issues may take several sessions. The important part is that you are transforming the team from a group of doers to a group of thinkers and forcing the concept of thoughtful planning and assessment. Involving the team serves another function as well. It creates an environment where others are holding each other accountable and there is a shared expectation of planning.

Your sphere of influence is not relegated to your immediate work team or department. Challenge everyone you come in contact with to be thinking strategically. Take every exchange opportunity to ask questions that are relevant to the next steps, but also open a conversation about the long-term opportunity or impact. The best mentors I have had always challenged me to think beyond the goal I had established in my mind about a given project. They took the opportunity to ask me how this related to my other projects or my overall vision for my department or entire organization. Regretfully, these conversations did not always result in having all the answers but they set me on a path of exploration and a desire to pursue excellence instead of just getting the task at hand completed and checked off my to-do list.

Refer to previous planning documents to make sure you are on (or off) track. The best planning processes have ended with concise documentation of the path ahead and key milestones. Ensure that you are not only preparing documents for external purposes or a one-time review. Take the time to create management plans and actionable outlines for each member of the team. Everyone should leave with an understanding of the immediate impact of the planning that has been done. This helps mitigate the risk that everyone returns to life as normal and the planning goes to waste. These action outlines and management plans also identify smaller milestones that can be assessed quickly so you can course correct sooner rather than later. It is never good to wait until that quarterly review of the plan and then realize that by week two you were off the path and could have made revisions months ago but that time is now lost.

If you do determine that you are off your original path, try to determine if there is good reason. These changes don't always signal a temporary detour but can mean a complete change to the path you have chosen. Understanding that there are multiple ways to arrive at a given destination will allow you to be flexible and will create a drive to always be on the best path—not just a path. You will need to be able to explain the change to your team, your board, your partners, and those you serve. Ensure that everyone is aware that the change is acknowledged and has been thought through. These types of changes should be decisions that are well thought out, assessed, and explained. Ask yourself why the need for the change and whether it is a temporary adjustment or one that could change the long-term path. Along with this diligence, you need to have the tools and resources available to make your planning meaningful and productive. The entire organization and the cause will benefit from the time spent on these efforts. While we spent a great deal of time planning for the wristband campaign, I feel more time discussing the potential and focusing on the larger impact would have been beneficial.

When we first learned about the opportunity with Nike our initial reaction was to start thinking through the details. Which web site will we direct people to? How soon with the wristbands arrive? We heard, "Let's sell five million wristbands" and our reaction was, "Great. Let's get started!" It was after talking with the rest of the leadership both inside the organization and our advisors externally that we started investigating the "What if?" For example, "What if we sell 10 million or 30 million instead of just five? What if Oprah encourages her listeners to buy bands? What if every student in the United States decides having a wristband is *the* fashion accessory the year?"

> "The future has several names.
> For the weak, it is the impossible.
> For the faint-hearted, it is the unknown. For the thoughtful and valiant, it is the ideal."
> —Victor Hugo

We were in planning mode from the beginning, but we were planning for wristband promotion and distribution. We were not planning for the impact on the organization, the potential of having five million people wearing wristbands, and how to activate them for the cause, or the potential long-term ramifications for the organization and the cancer community. We spent more time in the first few days asking "how to" questions instead of "what if." The Foundation hosted plenty of planning sessions but we tended to focus on logistics and more of the "how to" questions. If we needed to order more bands, how would we do it? The "how" of our plans were discussed in detail, but, overall, we could have done more to prepare for speaking opportunities, increased awareness, and calls to action along the way. An effective way to do this is with scenario planning. With scenario planning you can establish flexible, long-term plans that will uncovered hidden weaknesses and inflexibilities in the organization or its methods. You can think about the overall impact to the community you serve instead of distribution and logistics. Since the wristband campaign, the Foundation has continued to improve its scenario planning abilities and currently does a nice job of identifying the highest goal for a given project and building a plan from the top down. This is a much better approach instead of starting with the details and occasionally looking up.

While the wristband campaign was focused on the details, this was not the status quo within the organization and planning had always been a priority. Even during my interview process in the summer of 2000, I recall charting an organizational chart for the next three to five years with the board and advisors. As a team, we were continuously examining our progress and assessing the potential. Everyone had a sense that there was still so much untapped potential and we were eager to find a way to harness it. Our planning process and conversations were dramatically different post-wristband and our attention shifted from identifying and mobilizing the millions of cancer survivors we served to engaging our constituents in ways that would have lasting impact and how to leverage the success of LIVESTRONG.

The Planning Process

In 2005 we began our nine-month strategic planning process. We had hired a consultant who had experience transforming start-up organizations into mature, commercially viable companies. The planning process included all of the key stakeholders: the entire staff; the board; our advisors; our organization network; academia; government officials and advisors; and our partners. While each group did not participate in every meeting or discussion, there was a clear path of involvement for each audience. Work was done to establish the desired outcomes for each audience and how the results would be communicated and shared. During the planning, a few key themes emerged. Those themes included:

- creating a sense of balance;
- growing strategically;
- maintaining our organizational culture;
- impact and measurement; and,
- the need for a new goal for the organization.

In 2000, I remember conversations when the staff—all three of us—would discuss the possibility of having the attention of the world and being able to mobilize millions of survivors and help transform the Foundation from a small nonprofit to a global cancer organization creating real-world change. That was a tremendous goal and once we could see the impact of the wristband and its potential to help us achieve that goal, there was a need to verbalize our next Mount Everest. We were ready to plan for our next "big hairy audacious goal," as Jim Collins would say.

Gearing Up for the Planning Process

The process lasted nine months. It included several large group sessions, all staff meetings, department meetings, two executive retreats, a board retreat, a meeting of the leadership in the cancer community, and thousands of one-on-one conversations between the consultants, the management team, and with our constituents and partners. Our first priority was to decide on the key questions to be answered and the time and scope of the analysis. With the major stakeholders identified and engaged, we began mapping trends and identifying the key driving forces. While we were all actively participating in the strategic planning process, there were several conversations identifying the opportunities and bringing red flags and urgent decisions to the surface. Once we were able to discuss issues that were immediate and all agree to a plan of action, we could concentrate on the long-term planning. Our process had to be flexible with the team, because of the volume of activity at the time and the feeling that we could not wait and that the time was now to capture everything we could.

Each department was asked to evaluate its previous success, impact, and key drivers. The key-driver conversation was especially meaningful in the development department because it forced us to look at our revenue metrics differently. Instead of thinking about number of riders at the Ride for the Roses, we began an understanding of the true revenue drivers such as the top 10 percent of the riders. These key takeaways were informative and helped shaped future activities. Just forcing the conversation led to change and a deeper understanding of the organization and where our resources would best be applied.

Over the first six months, we identified potential scenarios, filtered and prioritized them, and examined those that seemed plausible. One of the best parts of the scenario planning exercise for me was the opportunity to think about the application of other models to what we were trying to accomplish. I have found that most nonprofit organizations operate within a very small sphere of influence. It is very easy to get tunnel vision and focus only on organizations within the same cause, region of the country, or fellow nonprofit organizations. Organizations do this while completely ignoring the fact that another cause, region, or for-profit may have been through something similar. There are lessons to be learned from their experience.

The scenario-planning exercises also highlighted those issues that were influential for the Foundation that we were unaware of or not tracking effectively. Trends in cycling, social networking adoption rates, creation of hundreds of nonprofits serving the survivorship audience, and other factors would have an impact for the organization. We needed to be ready to leverage these new opportunities. Scenario planning allowed us to think through our approach without being rushed. We were able to take our time, discuss every potential outcome and approach, and eventually come up with the best possible plan of action. Having these scenarios in place and really just having had the conversations around the possibilities was such a wonderful opportunity to get to know the team more closely, align our resources, understand where we fit into the larger landscape, and hone our skills for assessing these situations in the future as a team. We couldn't talk through every scenario that we could imagine so we needed to focus on those with the largest potential impact or that were of the most concern.

One of our biggest concerns at the time was that we would end up neglecting those we served—our constituents. We were able to have meaningful relationships with the survivors that we had come in contact with up to that point, but we could see that making that same level of high touch scalable could be a challenge. We discussed how we could avoid those situations in the future and what to do if they arose. On the positive side, we envisioned scenarios where there were multiple wristband-like campaigns being executed. We wanted to discuss how we would capture those opportunities when they presented themselves and leverage them to make a difference for those we were serving. Be wary of falling into the trap of being reactive and filtering incoming calls and requests, and getting distracted from taking the time to think proactively about who to partner with and when to approach them. Following the success of the LIVESTRONG wristband, the Foundation was receiving dozens of calls a week from organizations interested in partnership and the programs team was inundated with funding requests because of the new revenue being generated. If I were to go back, this would be one area I would change from the start. I would have allocated staff to the inbound calls but also would have dedicated more time to thinking about who was on our top prospect list that might be willing to talk to us during the height of the campaign that we were previously struggling to connect with. We needed to change our staffing structure and responsibilities. The Foundation has done an effective job of identifying those companies that have put a priority on customer service and entrepreneurial thinking like Zappos.com and Starbucks. They make a conscious effort to build relationships that have benefited the organization financially and provided countless hours of expertise and business insights as well.

The scenario-planning process itself allowed us to maintain a sense of balance at the organization. When reflecting on the strategic planning process in 2005, we needed to maintain a balance between being flexible—so we could take advantage of opportunities—and staying true to the organization's overarching goals. This is in line with the earlier idea of managing inbound calls from prospects while having a roadmap that we continued to execute regardless of what was incoming. And with the success of the wristband campaign came many new opportunities for development as well as programs.

We were asked by many people to leverage the LIVESTRONG brand to impact the larger health cause instead of staying focused on cancer. We were beginning to play a role in international advocacy and government outreach instead of being focused on making cancer a priority in the United States. Each staff member at the Foundation was making critical decisions each day that could influence the entire future of the organization. We needed to be on the same page and moving to the beat of the same drummer in order to ensure that our decisions would have positive long-term implications for the organization. When you are planning for the future of your organization, talk through all the possibilities including your worst fears and your highest hopes. Know that these planning exercises will result in much more than a binder on the shelf and that the process itself will be a great source of strength and confidence as you lead later on.

Determining the Appropriate Planning Process for Your Organization

Why stop to plan? Things were going well and calls were constantly coming in for more revenue opportunities and potential program partners. Wasn't this what we had worked for? Was this the time to sit back and just let it all happen? I credit our Board of Directors with the decision to bring in the expertise at this moment in the organization's maturity. We had conducted several planning sessions through the years but this was different. There was a sense of obligation and duty to seize the moment—carpe diem. Things were taking off and the time was now to really accelerate the momentum and do more. When you are determining whether you need a strategic plan, business plan, management plan, or a little of everything, a few questions to consider include:

- What questions are we trying to answer?
- Does everyone know the larger strategic goals of the organization and can they articulate them effectively?
- Do we have timelines and measurements in place to determine our progress toward our goals?

- Where are we succeeding currently and where do we seem to be lacking?
- Currently, who could or should be involved in a planning process?
- What is the desired outcome of the planning?
- What audiences will need to be addressed during and after planning?
- What resources do we have to manage the planning project and where are there gaps?
- Is the organization ready to participate in the planning process?
- Are we going to be willing to act upon the recommendations even if they mean serious personal career changes for various individuals?
- What education needs to be done with the staff prior to launching the planning so everyone understands the process and values the opportunity?

In 2005, the answers we provided to these questions led us to begin the nine-month strategic planning process. At the Foundation, we were trying to answer the question of "what's next?" What does a post-wristband future look like for the organization and are we effectively leveraging this to its full potential? We also needed to understand the state of the organization and where we were lacking both in infrastructure, talent, and operations. Everyone at the Foundation was aware of our mission at the time we launched the planning process, but there was still opportunity to refine our programmatic focus and better communicate those survivorship goals to the general public. Without the planning, we would have continued on a very straight and thankfully upward trend based on past

performance, but we wouldn't be planning for something different—something better. We needed timelines
and metrics for the growth we wanted instead of the
growth that would just naturally happen based on
the past. We had a first-rate group of staff members,
board members, advisors, survivors, and corporate
and program partners. We needed to take the time
to engage each group in the future of the Foundation
and harness their collective knowledge and excitement.
We hoped that the outcome of the planning process
would be a more mature, visionary organization. If
we were a for-profit, we would have been preparing
the organization to be acquired, go public, or expand
exponentially. Many of our board members were
venture capitalists and they were also our largest donors.
They were interested in the social return on investment
and in true venture-capital style, they were not only
providing us with the financial capital to grow our
organization, they were also providing the mentorship
and guidance to take advantage of the ever-evolving
opportunities at the Foundation.

Understanding the answers to these questions and
having a basic understanding of the applicability of
these planning tools is the responsibility of all leaders
within an organization. Leaders need to think about
when and how to apply these tools for maximum
impact. Not every project or partnership needs a nine-
month planning process. There were plenty of meetings
where we would simply gather a group of key stakeholders for a two-hour prioritization meeting or gather
input on a new opportunity so we could plan while
keeping all potential impacts in mind. The important
commonality here is that there was a focus on the

planning and purposeful intent with every opportunity. These planning exercises, great or small, allow those involved to address the fundamental issues facing the organization and truly make a change and learn from the process itself.

Creating a Roadmap: You Are Here

When creating a roadmap for the future for your organization and the potential impact of a campaign, you need to understand where you have been, where you are currently, and identify the forces that can influence where you are headed in the future. Scenario planning can be a valuable tool when developing your roadmap. Writing scenarios about the future requires a historical review of the organization, but also a basic review of the present—an understanding of where you are now on the map. This assessment of your current situation should include the evolution of the organization's vision, mission, and goals and their current state.

The Lance Armstrong Foundation's mission evolved from helping people with testicular cancer to all urological cancers and eventually became a resource for all cancers. In the early 2000s, the Foundation hosted a series of meetings with leading researchers, cancer nonprofit executives, government officials, and advisors and ended up with the determination that the Foundation's real potential was in serving cancer survivors at the point of diagnosis and beyond. This meant we would not be addressing prevention, education, and screening but rather seeking to impact people's lives after they had been told "You have cancer." The

Foundation's focus allowed us to galvanize the tens of millions of survivors that had felt unconnected and underserved because once their treatment was complete they were no longer able to take part in the services and programs afforded to them during treatment. The Foundation understood that once a person is diagnosed, it changes everything including fertility, career, insurance rights, geography, future health concerns, and more. Having an understanding of this past and where the Foundation was in 2005 was important to creating our path for the future. It required an openness and interest in the history of the organization and an appreciation for the organic growth in the early years. It also provided insights into the strengths and weaknesses of the Foundation through the years.

Doing a SWOT (strengths, weaknesses, opportunities, and threats) analysis is a must during the planning process. This is true for planning at every level and for any reason. This past year I was advising a client dealing with chapter-relations concerns. There had been an exorbitant amount of dialogue about the issues but progress had not been made. The first conversation I facilitated with the national office team was a SWOT analysis. We quickly uncovered the opportunities but also were able to use the threats and weaknesses to filter those opportunities we could influence immediately. Once the SWOT was complete we had a set of short- and long-term objectives and could begin discussing appropriate action plans.

Another use of SWOT analysis is to create an inventory of the assets you have to offer potential partners. Use your SWOT assessments to identify new opportunities and be realistic about which ones you

"An entrepreneur is someone willing to go out on a limb, having it cut off behind her, and discovering she had wings all the time."
—Leigh Thomas

pursue. And do not try to do a SWOT analysis with a small and internal group of people. Be sure to validate your analysis with other key stakeholders. This is a great way to engage people on an on-going basis in your planning and can be a very quick and effective way for them to provide input and substantially impact the outcomes of the process.

Along with the SWOT analysis, consider involving your outside partners in the scenario-planning process. In hindsight, it would have been interesting to ask the two primary teams from the wristband campaign, Nike and Foundation, to write three different stories based around a set of mutually agreed upon themes. It would have been very helpful to think about a scenario where the Foundation opened LIVESTRONG retail outlets. Or, how we would have imagined the brand evolving given the increase in social media and how we could leverage it. The Foundation's programs team could have shared insights with the cancer community to contemplate the potential for more cancer treatments that would lead to longer-term survivorship issues and opportunities to serve our constituents. Hearing various scenarios and discussing the ever-changing landscape helps provide cross-team insights and sparks ideas. Giving each person three potential scenarios would have been one way to start the dialogue.

During your planning, consider scenarios that incorporate the following:

- legal changes including donor restrictions or changes that cause companies to distribute their philanthropic dollars differently;
- nonprofit consolidation;
- giving trends;
- (if health related) changes in diagnosis rates, screening, or treatments;
- communication channel evolution; or,
- rapid events growth.

The potential scenarios are countless. The important thing is to select a few that everyone can agree will be an influencing factor in your organization's future. The scenarios chosen should be plausible and include relevant forces or drivers. A way to quickly generate a list of potential scenarios is to start asking the question "what if?"

Using this to your advantage by thinking through all the possibilities will enable you to be more prepared. You can identify the processes that need to be in place, outline the decision tree, and understand how the organization will react in a time of opportunity or when there is a need for urgency. In hindsight, asking more "what if" questions would have been helpful for the various teams involved in the LIVESTRONG campaign. Even when time was tight and deadlines were near, stopping to ask "what if?" could have saved us hours when dealing with staffing issues, branding concerns, backorders, and more. Had we gone through these exercises more diligently, we could have identified the key drivers and influenced those more effectively at every stage of the process.

Identifying Key Drivers

A campaign the size of LIVESTRONG included so many variables from the start that we had to map out the drivers in order to take action in a number of areas. A key driver is a factor that determines the success or failure of an organization's strategy. An important question to ask when planning a new project is "what are the key drivers?" When reflecting on the success of the LIVESTRONG wristband campaign, questions we asked ourselves included:

> *"The best way to predict the future is to create it."*
> —Stephen R. Covey

- Did the celebrities drive success?
- Were the cancer survivors in the hospitals the ones that drove demand?
- Were the efforts made in leveraging our grassroots program partners effective?
- Was Lance's appearance on Oprah the tipping point?
- Could we have achieved this same success without the Olympics and the U.S. presidential race going on in the same year?
- Was Lance winning the tour that year critical to the success of the overall campaign?
- Was it essential to have both online and in-store sales available?

• Was the fashion industry engagement important in increasing demand for the audience that had not already been directly impacted by our cause?

As I've mentioned previously, in the instance of LIVESTRONG, every lever was being pushed at full throttle and we were operating under a general sense of "let's see what happens." Thankfully it worked. However, could we have accomplished as much with less? If we tried to repeat it, would we need to do everything the same as we did in 2004? What would we do differently? What could we have done without? I believe that repetition of the wristband campaign would require the same energies and outreach. We benefited from a ground swell of activity and excitement coming from multiple channels. If we had not made the government officials a target audience for wristband outreach, the presidential candidates would not have been wearing the band and the idea of "cancer as a national priority" would not have been mentioned during presidential debates. The Olympics provided an opportunity for Nike to leverage every athlete, not just the typical professional athletes, and give them a chance to get involved and show a sense of solidarity on a global scale. Lance's win allowed the campaign to go beyond July 2004 and created additional buzz and momentum as a way to acknowledge such an amazing feat. I believe we would work to replicate the campaign exactly as it was executed. It was planned and deliberate, but flexible enough to grow organically and take advantage of every new opportunity. We would need to add new components for social media outreach and more global elements to address the ever-expanding reach of the organization, but overall there is not an element of the campaign that I would recommend dismissing or that I believe did not directly impact the outcome in a substantial way. I would also leave out those items we intentionally removed from the plan because I believe they still would not have been as impactful in reaching the overall goals. One example of this was the allocation of media dollars to a print and TV media budget. With the support of Nike and the opportunity to speak to people on the community level, a large media buy was not in line with our campaign vision and may have just been noise in the background and not produced real tangible results.

Identifying the key drivers, those you want to pursue and those you feel should be dismissed, can be a daunting task. There are so many choices of activities and focus it is hard to decide which will have the most influence and be most impactful. There are various methods for determining the key drivers. One tool I use frequently is the Five Whys.

Tools for Finding Out "Why"

When you are creating a plan and trying to understand where to allocate your limited resources, asking "why" can provide keen insights for your future decision making. As I said earlier, if you think scenario planning sounds like some type of long, extensive planning program, think again. Tools like the Five Whys or storytelling through visualization and communication can give you a quick and easy-to-implement way to get started.

For instance, the Five Whys technique requires "Why?" be asked of each response or sub-case until the core cause is reached. Usually this takes five times of asking someone "why," but it could take more or less, depending on the issue at hand. This is also a great tool to use when considering a new potential partner. It can help you get to the one-sentence description of the partnership or determine if the partnership is even a good fit for your organization. You can leverage the knowledge and insights gained from the process to engage others and get them to buy into your vision. With this information, they are more likely to take an active role in the success of the campaign.

I am currently working with the Austin Film Society (AFS) to determine the best usage of the National Guard Armory building that will become available to the AFS in the fall of 2012. The initial concept was to develop the space into a Creative Media Hub. Along with town hall meetings with the film and education industries, advisory group sessions, online discussion forums, and external model research, we have utilized the Five Whys exercise. It has helped us streamline our messaging for various audiences. There is a wide range of individuals and organizations that must be engaged and enthusiastic about the project in order to secure the necessary funding and to be invested in the project long-term. The following is the result of the Five Whys exercise:

Austin Needs a Creative Media Hub
Why?
Because our creative industry currently located in the city feels disparate and there is an opportunity

cost involved in missing out on opportunities to convene and influence this segment of our community.

Why?

Encouraging creativity and facilitating creative-based entrepreneurship and business support is beneficial for every Central Texas citizen and for the entire creative industry.

Why?

The culture of Austin is positively impacted by having a thriving and organized creative industry. It makes Austin a place where people want to live and work. It also attracts creative professionals who want to feel valued and contribute to the communities that are making an investment in their skills and talents.

Why?

Providing a unique city positively influences our combined sense of community and our ability to attract and retain quality individuals, families, and businesses in Austin. And economic growth impacts our ability to deliver quality infrastructure to our residents including programs such as education.

Why?

If we don't build on the momentum of the Austin Film Society and the growth the city's creative industry, we will begin losing talented members of our community to other cities and our window of opportunity to convene and serve as a catalyst may be lost. Innovative and influential people want to be at the epicenter of activity and surround themselves with people and places of influence and action. Infrastructure and community growth ensure long-term viability to the region and an increase in potential investment in future community enhancements.

By asking the Five Whys, we uncovered the problem statement, potential opportunity costs to be factored into the project, and the positive cultural aspect of developing the Creative Media Hub, as well as the economic impact for the project. We also realized the impact of the facility on corporate recruitment, education, and city growth. These statements will be valuable when drafting the key messaging statements and understanding our potential audiences and areas of influence within the community.

Another useful tool is visualization. At your next development-team meeting, invite everyone to simply close their eyes and visualize what the desired state of the organization accomplishing its goal might be like. They should consider questions like:

• What will the organization look like when it has 10 corporate partners engaged?
• What will be different when the multimedia fund-raising campaign reaches every state?

Once you and your team have a vision for what may occur, you can start to think through the logistics of supporting that outcome. Likely, it will be a hybrid of the team members' visions. By sharing and talking through each scenario together, the organization can be best prepared to deal with whatever reality unfolds.

"The world is an ambiguous place. As a leader of a NPO and someone trying to create change in the world, you better have tolerance for ambiguity, because if you don't you will get stuck on your path and get in a rut and those opportunities will pass you by."

—Randall Macon

One of the most useful tools in scenario planning toward accomplishing your goals is communication among team members. It does not help the organization or your partners if you go through planning exercises and don't share the fruits and outcomes of the discussions with every individual who could potentially be impacted.

Communication must be required of the team handling planning efforts. Tools to implement open communication can be as simple as reporting during weekly meetings, or as complicated as building an entire web site around the planning activities. Be sure to include the original questions and answers that are being developed and determine what communication tools are appropriate given the scope of your organization's specific opportunity at the time.

To this end, consider implementing planning tools such as a planning room or display boards to highlight current thinking and continually ask questions. At the Foundation, we used four six-foot tall pieces of black mounting board from a local art store. We would print and display meeting reports, new charts or graphs that were being developed, and updates to the planning timeline. You can also utilize a white board that stays stationary throughout the process so people can provide input and ideas if they are so inclined. Having everything stored on the organization's intranet or sharing documents with online document sharing technology is important because these documents and tracking will be essential during the final stages of writing and producing the plan. But do not underestimate the power of seeing these ideas and insights live and in person. Remember that no one wants to read 60 pages of slides or text. Information should be condensed so that people have the most important takeaways. The final plan should be comprehensive and provide the action items, key takeaways, and the overview of the process that lead to these conclusions, but making the process accessible and tangible cannot be overlooked. These display methods allow key takeaways to be easily understood and implemented.

Whether it is traditional scenario planning or using one of the other methods mentioned here, any investment of time in planning and thinking about future potential impacts requires everyone to listen and communicate and appreciate each others' ideas. Find the methods that are right for your organization and get started. Every member of your organization, inside and out, will be impacted by the time and energy put into strategic planning. These efforts will result in more cohesive and effective teams and can positively impact team morale.

No Department (or Colleague) Left Behind

Individual departments or teams can participate in planning sessions and utilize exercises like the Five Whys or scenario planning, but spheres of influence should always be a consideration. When you are conducting planning exercises or projects, be sure to think about the impact of your outcomes and goal to every group you influence. For the fundraising department this typically includes finance, marketing, and operations. Consider each area and department of your organization. When going through scenario-planning exercises, think not only about operations, fundraising, and marketing but also the potential impact to mission and services. During the LIVESTRONG campaign, for example, Doug and his programs team worked quickly to keep up with the increased demand for support from cancer survivors and the new grant requests coming in every day. If we had spent more time with the programs team conducting a planning exercise, we might have highlighted this potential outcome and had a plan in place to address the increased demand for services. Our focus with the mission team was distribution of wristbands, not increased survivor requests. We involved the programs team in some aspects of the campaign but left them on their own regarding scalability planning.

This same situation happened in the marketing department: The Foundation's Director of Marketing and Communication, who was at the Foundation from 2000 to 2007, reflected on how more planning might have been helpful for her department. She said it would have been helpful to understand the potential need for turn-key media response resources of people and tools. Her team had spent their time on how to pitch the story and working to get people excited about the campaign. She felt we could have done more to be prepared for the incoming media requests. We had not planned for what would be needed from the Marketing and Communication Department once we had reached the tipping point or achieved critical mass with the wristbands.

We could have discussed the transition from outgoing media outreach to managing incoming media opportunities and information requests. We didn't necessarily leave the Marketing and Communication team on their own, but we could have helped each other identify potential pivotal moments in the campaign and planned accordingly.

> *"If you want to be happy, put your effort into controlling the sail, not the wind."*
> —Anonymous

The key takeaway is that an integral part of strategic planning, or planning at any level, involves thinking about each key stakeholder, especially the various departments in your organization, and asking how they might be impacted and how they can best prepare and have a positive influence on the outcomes. When you find the right solution or a campaign that resonates with your audience, the demand will be so tremendous that your entire organization must be ready to respond accordingly. Remember, be positive and ask "what if?"

I also wanted to make a special note about the fact that scenario planning is not only applicable to organizations or campaigns but also to individuals. The tools presented here are good for groups but also for you as an individual contributor to the team. When you are presented with a new situation, it is only natural to ask "what about me?" or "how will this impact me?" Take time to think about how your specific role will be impacted and how you want to address those challenges and opportunities. If your team sees you taking the time to be thoughtful at every level, organization-wide and individually, you will set the standard for the type of purposeful and effective work you expect from those around you. It will help you identify key milestones throughout the campaign to monitor your success and also to celebrate achievements along the way.

Pinpointing the Decision Points

The idea of monitoring your success and progress through the process is not only for the individual but for the entire team. Reporting dashboards and key metrics are essential pieces of information and serve as on-going reminders of the plan and organization's long-term goal. These timelines can also contain information about key decision milestones. Once you have identified key decisions that need to be made, you can plan ahead and develop the decision protocols, determine accountability and ensure proper processes. As discussed above, involving both programs and marketing departments were essential to the success of the campaign and both groups were drastically influenced by the launch and success of the wristband campaign. Along with these teams, we also needed to consider infrastructure including supply chain management, operations, integration with finance, and legal implications. If we had spent more time with these departments I would have hoped to uncover critical decision points in the process.

Without the proper planning for a campaign of any size, there can be a sense of anxiety about the unknown that fills every conversation. With some additional planning and discussion you can identify these key decision points and reduce the anxiety around the process.

In the first few days of the pre-planning for the wristband campaign, a large number of decisions were made. We determined everything from what data to capture when people ordered bands online to how we would overcome shipping charges being more than the cost of a single band (we offered them in packs of 10 online). We made decisions as we became aware of the issues and at that point people were still available to thoughtfully consider various options. As the campaign got under way and a general sense of urgency took over both Nike and the Foundation, we missed the opportunity to set a process in place for how and when we would make future decisions and answer questions like:

- Who would be responsible for making the final call on wristband re-orders?
- What triggers would influence the re-order process?
- What approvals needed to be secured in order to place re-orders?

Key campaign decisions happened every hour during the LIVESTRONG campaign. With more planning on the front end of your campaign, you can have a greater sense of assurance that the decisions being made are right or at least that you have gone through the proper steps to determine the decision and have a better chance the decision will be correct. Assessing these key decision milestones also provides for more flexibility long term because the individuals responsible for the decisions when the time comes know how to react and can do so nimbly and without hesitation. Planning allows an organization to adapt and be ready when the opportunity presents itself and should not be seen as a level of red tape or unnecessary structure.

"In an environment of change, you don't want a very rigid organizational structure. You want one that allows you to adapt."

—Michael Hammer

Don't Stop (Especially When Things Are Going Well)

As I mentioned earlier, we began our strategic planning process in 2005, during the height of the wristband campaign. Just when many groups would have been relaxing and celebrating, we were setting our sights on new horizons and looking for areas of improvement and opportunity. As the campaign continued, operations became smoother. We had dealt with the issues of international shipping and backorders, increased the number of wristband suppliers, created new partner resources, added new merchandise expertise to the team, and had made our overall operations more scalable and efficient. We were revising our programmatic outreach and funding and the new strategy was ensuring the maximum amount of impact for the dollars being distributed. This is where we could have quickly become mired in the details and the future campaign execution. However, the organization once again made a wise choice and allocated more members of the team to forward-facing initiatives. As the campaign continued to grow, we started dedicating more resources and attention to the new future of LIVESTRONG. In 2005, Randall Macon and Tiffany Galligan were promoted to the newly created Department of Innovation and I moved into the position of director of new business within the Development Department. The three of us spent our time understanding the key business drivers including revenue and assessing future roadmap options. We started by looking at existing and proposed programs and possible organization extensions. With an influx of resources including money and an increased interest in the cause by volunteers, survivors, vendors, partners, and individuals, we started to think again about the possibilities and the potential for LIVESTRONG. This was a different type of planning because typically, the organization had been focused on projects that would influence the organization within the next quarter or year. The projects we worked on in these departments were intended for long-term application of five years plus. And, even though we were charting our course for the long-term future, it took me some time to adjust to the notion that while a specific path that had been outlined and might be ideal, there is no telling how everything will end up. Everyone had to have a willingness to adjust and be adaptable.

Entrepreneurs are often forced to move forward with an unmatched level of passion and commitment, but also need to be honest and humble enough to know there may be another, better path or model uncovered in the future. Being willing to admit that there might be a better way and a willingness to explore it will make you a much more valuable asset for any organization or cause than someone who is taking a plan set previously and executing without deviation. A strategic plan is a roadmap. It serves as a guide. It should not be impenetrable and should be constantly evaluated by those carrying out the plan. Assuming everything you implement today will stay the same one month or one year from now is not wise. New information constantly comes to light during the life of campaigns. When other models become available to you, arrogance can kill progress. It's always better to embrace the unknown and acknowledge the need to continuously improve and answer questions. If you have done your homework and planning, you will be ready for whatever comes your way.

> *"The crowd lives in comfort. An extraordinary life thrives in testing the limit. Let the testing begin."*
> —Scott Dinsmore

★　　★　　★

The Lance Armstrong Foundation and Nike made many wise decisions, small and large, throughout the

LIVESTRONG campaign. Poor decisions or a general lack of interest in the goals could have led to complete failure of the campaign. Fortunately, the combination of our decisions and the timing of the campaign led to absolute success. We identified the mission-critical decisions early on and made those activities a priority. We made revenue reporting a high priority. Be sure you understand the legal implications of the campaign prior to the launch with the help of outside counsel and board members. The Foundation understood the importance of making this campaign accessible to everyone including grantees, partners, advocates, and donors. We knew we couldn't accomplish the sale of five million wristbands alone. It took planning and preparation to engage each of these constituents in a meaningful and impactful way.

> *"Integrity is usually lost in small choices, the ones that seem insignificant at the time. Most people do not make a conscious decision to sacrifice their integrity by making one big, bad mistake. It is the accumulation of bad choices, all of which seem minor, that leads to the next bad choice."*
> —David Cottrell

It's important to remember, too, that any time people dedicate themselves to a cause greater than any one person or organization, there is a level of sacrifice that is required. Acknowledging the sacrifice can prevent feelings of being over-worked or experiencing rapid burn out. When working on a campaign like the LIVESTRONG wristband, be prepared to put in overtime—and not just weeknights. I once gave a presentation with a member of the team at Nike at the Cause Marketing Forum. One of the presentation slides was simply a picture of an alarm clock that read 3:00 a.m. The campaign took over everything, even our dreams.

"Change is the essence of life. Be willing to surrender what you are for what you could become."
—Mahatma Gandhi

Overall, strategic planning allows you to run through the potential outcomes and pre-determine the answers to the many detailed questions involved in a project, so you and your colleagues don't get lost along the way.

Be sure to also give yourself a little time to test your theories and roadmaps. Find opportunities to pilot everything and do this with the knowledge that revisions are the standard and not the exception. This will afford you the opportunity to discover problems and find solutions. The things you learn when testing out ideas and initiatives also helps strengthen the relationships and processes that you could end up using for months (or years) to come.

Again, be sure that learning from these opportunities is a priority for the whole team. Every area can potentially be impacted from these experiments. No one person can be responsible for identifying every segment of the campaign that needs to be addressed or modified. The Foundation was a team of leaders. Establishing cross-functional teams on a variety of projects prior to the wristband campaign allowed the organization to mobilize effectively when the time came with Nike. The Foundation was no longer its own team but rather part of a larger group of individuals and organizations working toward one common goal. Recognizing all of the teams your organization is a part of can be the first step to assessing your value on those teams and understanding how you can improve them and make an impact.

Chapter 6

Assembling the Perfect Team

One of the most influential components of the LIVESTRONG campaign for me personally was the ability to work with an amazing team of colleagues; the absolute best team in the world. Everyone brought their A game to the campaign. We were all motivated by the idea that this campaign might just change the entire cancer community in a way that none of

> *"Surround yourself with people who are optimistic and caring; it's one time when being 'surrounded' is a good thing."*
>
> —Al Lucia

us could have imagined previously. In every meeting, every conversation, and every email there was a sense that history was in the making. And after working on LIVESTRONG, everyone was thankful to have played a part, no matter how big or small.

Many of the people that worked on the wristband campaign had been with the Lance Armstrong Foundation (Foundation) for a number of years. Bianca, Randall, Doug, the development team, and many of the board members helped prepare the organization for the opportunity LIVESTRONG presented. Their knowledge of the relationships we could leverage to make the campaign a success was invaluable. Our teamwork and mutual respect—honed over time and previous projects—also played a huge part in the success and enthusiasm of the LIVESTRONG campaign.

> *"Things may come to those who wait, but only the things left by those who hustle."*
>
> —Abraham Lincoln

Since starting work on the project in 2004, the Foundation gave me the opportunity to work with a sense of purpose and within an organization willing to try new things. The Foundation wanted to not just move the needle but really turn everything upside down. It was such a gift and I will be forever grateful for having the experience. And I am humbled by having the opportunity of working with Lance, as well.

Every LIVESTRONG team member did their part. The evolution of each person's role within the Foundation played into the success and impact on the campaign. For example, Bianca Bellavia was leading the Marketing and Communication Department in 2004 but previously had been the Peloton Project Manager and oversaw other development efforts. Because of her knowledge of the fundraising side of the business, she was always looking for ways to utilize her marketing and communication efforts to generate additional dollars or serve as an acquisition tool. Had we been working with a media relations person or marketing manager that had never been exposed to fundraising and its fundamentals, we might have missed several opportunities that resulted in significant impact for the Foundation.

Our Cause Marketing Manager, Jeff Manning, joined us in 2003. Jeff had previous experience with retail and athletic apparel companies as a member of the corporate sponsorship team at the Red Sox and for The Jimmy Fund. Working closely with Jeff was Kevin Filo and they both were invaluable to the campaign. As you are building a team, be sure to evaluate not only the current needs of the organization but also the areas where you would like to expand and when an opportunity comes up, assess the backgrounds and passions of existing team members. There may be a chance that the person working on your endowment efforts happened to work at a partner organization previously and could lend insight to your campaign or some similar situation. I think all of this information is relevant because it really should beg the question, what are the backgrounds of the people on our team currently and how are we leveraging that experience and knowledge?

Everyone in the organization was involved in the campaign. There was no time for programs versus

"There is one thing worse than training people and losing them, and that's not training them and keeping them."
—Zig Ziglar

fundraising or marketing versus accounting. In order for something as large as the campaign to evolve, it wasn't—and couldn't be—one person's pet project. Campaigns like LIVESTRONG must involve an entire team so everyone can leverage what is happening in their own special way to benefit the whole organization. In a time of silos and national versus chapters, truly powerful campaigns can only happen when everyone is on the same team and truly mission driven.

One of the things that I believe set us apart from other organizations was that we were a group of leaders. No one was standing around waiting for a job description to tell them what needed to be done. Everyone worked smartly and efficiently to move the organization forward. We were not an organization being led by one charismatic leader. We were a group of leaders producing major change.

Board of Directors

Lance was always good about surrounding himself with strong people—the best of the best. He expected a tremendous amount of investment by the Foundation leaders. Our Board of Directors was a strong group of people with whom I was privileged to work. They truly helped guide our staff not just in an advisory capacity but also tactically and strategically. Within the Board of

Directors there was a core group of advisors that served as the guiding force for the organization. Every member's commitment was visible and their hands-on approaches raised the bar for everything that was produced.

"As a board member, you have an opportunity to be significant, not just successful."
—Jeff Garvey

After establishing a clear vision born from planning and communication, it was easy to engage the leaders throughout our organization to take charge and make decisions that were best for moving forward toward our shared goal. The strength of our Board was a huge asset for the Foundation. Invest time and energy in creating relationships with your Board and facilitate its interaction. Board members are eager to learn from one another. Engaging them with new opportunities available to the organization is key to the success of potential strategies and initiatives. When something as large as what happened with the LIVESTRONG wristband campaign comes to fruition, your board will be essential in keeping things moving and making new things happen. You can also utilize allies among the various leadership groups to help secure support for campaign concepts and partnerships. The board can be the greatest group of people on earth or they can make progress within your department impossible. Take the time to engage them early in your work so they can be involved from the start—not just when you have to have their support to pass a potential partnership.

As a group, the LIVESTRONG team engendered a culture of "compulsive communication." We talked about everything, spent weekends together, were in book clubs with our co-workers and their spouses, and attended each other's weddings and special occasions. In the early days, three or four of us shared an office intended for one, so communicating was a little simpler then. But as we expanded into larger office spaces, there wasn't a day that went by when you couldn't find someone standing in an office doorway talking about a new idea or asking for input on a topic or task. We freely communicated our wishes and desires for the Foundation to anyone who would listen, both internally and externally. We believed enlisting people in the cause was the only way to accomplish our goals. We knew our vision wouldn't be possible with a staff of three, 16, or even 50. We needed everyone to go out into the world and make the vision a reality.

A Leader of Leaders

In *Rethinking the Future*,[1] Warren Bennis says:

> "Leaders of federations don't think of their associates as 'troops'. And the associates don't think of their leaders as generals. The leader of the new federal corporation has to be a leader of leaders . . . you have to create an environment in which other leaders, who subscribe to your vision, can make effective decisions themselves. An environment in which people at all levels are empowered to be leaders. . . . It's about creating a shared sense of purpose."

[1] *Rethinking the Future: Rethinking Business, Principles, Competition, Control & Complexity, Leadership, Markets, and the World*. Rowan Gibson. London, Nicholas Brealey Publishing, 1998.

An organization's leadership, not just the management, needs to be strong if the organization is going to be strong and make an impact. A few questions you might ask when evaluating your organization include:

- Is your organization under strong leadership?
- Knowing that every single colleague in an organization can improve, what can be done to improve leadership within your organization?
- What is your plan to improve leadership in your organization?
- What can you do to improve your leadership abilities?

There is opportunity everywhere for leadership improvement. One segment of the nonprofit landscape that could benefit from additional efforts in this area is national organizations with a chapter structure. The division between the national office and chapters can cause the greatest cause-marketing campaign in the world to fail miserably. On the other hand, when the entire organization, national and local offices, works together to offer value to a partner, delivers partnership benefits, and seeks to go above and beyond, knowing that greater involvement is possible, it can be very attractive to a potential partner. Discussing corporate outreach initiatives in general terms and agreeing to the operations systems, revenue distribution, database ownership, project management, and more can set the tone for a stronger working relationship when an actual company wants to get involved nationally. It also provides an opportunity to create a cross-functional work team and results will be more likely if the team has worked together to solve significant issues in the past. This is also a situation where over-communication is helpful. Within any one chapter office there are a million things to get done on a daily basis. It is easy for the management team at the chapter to get very focused on the tasks at hand and lose sight of how their work relates to the larger organization and the shared mission. And it is equally easy for a national organization to be focused on pursuing new opportunities and forget to include the rest of the organization in those conversations at the right moments. The issue I see is that the only solutions really being considered to solve these problems are nonprofit ways of thinking.

A close friend of mine works within a large retail organization. She spends her days representing the company to the local and regional managers and directors that are on the front lines engaging with the customers and supporting the stores. Sometimes, she will share work challenges or exciting new concepts. Many of her challenges sound similar to the complaints and concerns of these national chapter-based organizations. The tools they have created and the systems they use to make the operations run efficiently sound very close to the nonprofits mentioned above. I challenge every nonprofit to take away the concept of for-profit or nonprofit and simply examine the business model they are currently using. Once that has been identified, look for other organizations that are using a similar model. How are they handling these issues? Would they be willing to share some insights, tools, or advice? Do not try to re-create the wheel and it is silly to think that only your organization is dealing with these very issues. Building your team is key to all future success, so don't think about small process improvements but rather try to find those things that can transform the organization and make real lasting change.

Recognizing Red Flags

I do not want to mislead anyone into thinking that there is some perfect solution that will make all of your troubles disappear and the cause-marketing gates will open wide and all the benefits will just start pouring in. While the experiences I'm describing on the LIVESTRONG campaign all sound like it was some kind of non-profit Shangri-la, we did have our share of challenges. At times, the organization would get overly complicated and systems or process improvements would take precedence over action. I believe this is one of the places where our founder had a huge impact.

Lance is a huge fan of people that get things done. He appreciates it, he fosters it, and he will do his best to help in removing any obstacles standing in the way. We could always count on Lance to ask questions that would cut through the clutter and focus on the real deliverable. Lance is a believer of keeping things simple yet effective and that spirit filtered through his organization. After presenting new corporate partner opportunities including the case for support and projecting potential outcomes, Lance would simply ask, "Do they genuinely care about people with cancer?" If the answer was yes and the connection to the cause could be explained, he would just nod and you knew that you had the green light to move forward. No hoops or crazy analysis—just understanding their motivation and harnessing that to make a difference.

That focus on moving this forward efficiently transferred to the implementation of cause-marketing campaigns as well. He would be excited about a new campaign or relationship and wanted to start sharing the news with the masses immediately so he would call or email for updates during planning. His emails would always serve to light a little fire under the team—if he was excited, we were anxious to get it out to the market and start spreading the word.

While Lance was always excited about these new programs, he usually seemed surprised. He would often ask, "Why would they do all of that for us?" or wonder if anyone would show up for an event or purchase the Foundation-branded item over others. He was very humble and did not assume things would just work out. He wanted to know how we would put the pieces in place before the launch to ensure us the best possible chance for success. On a personal note, I remember when we were preparing for one of Lance's welcome home events following a Tour de France win. The City of Austin was planning to have a concert downtown including live music, a massive stage, vendors, celebrity guest appearances, and more. As I described all of this to Lance, his only response was, "Do you think anyone will show up?" Fascinating.

While he was humble and grateful for every opportunity to raise funds and awareness for the Foundation, he was also the first person to pick up the phone and call if he saw something he didn't like about a campaign or use of the Foundation's name that contradicted his vision. He could be counted on to raise the red flags that others might not be brave enough to bring to the attention of the team. This inspired others to speak up and not just let things happen but stop them along the way, make improvements or changes, and move onto the next opportunity. Take a lesson from his playbook and ask the tough questions. Every team needs someone to play devil's advocate and the risk of every new venture needs to be evaluated in order to make informed decisions about how and when to move forward with the opportunity or partnership.

> *"Never be afraid to try something new. Remember, amateurs built the ark. Professionals built the Titanic."*
> —Anonymous

There was a tremendous need for red flags postwristband. Once the wristband became a success and the LIVESTRONG brand was sought after by companies and partners of every kind, the team needed to assess each opportunity effectively and with careful examination. The strength of the leadership was making sure we did not lose our sense of purpose. The Foundation was growing like crazy, and a lot of time and attention was spent just trying to keep up. Advisors from every corner of the earth seemed to be imparting their knowledge and recommendations to the Board, our executive management team, and every member of the campaign staff. Some of this resulted in a change in our organization structure and management. Often this is a necessary phase in the evolution of an organization in order to grow but, it can slow things down a bit and not always in a good way.

Remember that these skills, assets, personalities, and relationships were instrumental in securing these growth opportunities to begin with. It is part of what attracted the two partners to each other and made it a success. Knowing that the value of the original mission or goals hasn't changed is an important touchstone that should not be modified without significant consideration by people who have shown their dedication and support to the cause. Maintaining the mission as the organization explodes may take support by more operations expertise or services, but be wary of expansion that simply adds a layer of management.

For instance, along with our internal teams, the vendors supporting the Foundation played a critical part in the LIVESTRONG campaign. We could not have executed a campaign of its magnitude without them, especially as the campaign continued to expand. Many of our vendors had been long-time supporters of the Foundation and had great relationships with our staff and volunteers. Having those relationships in place prior to the launch was integral. As the Foundation grew, it sometimes struggled to find the right people or organizations to fill a need. But identifying a process for generating new relationships with potential staff, contractors, and suppliers should be a priority long before the actual needs arise.

> *"Your life is not important except for the impact it has on another life."*
>
> —Jackie Robinson

Further, when interacting with different teams, especially at such a fast pace, one of the lessons I have learned is that as soon as you know something is not right, make a change. If you find you are putting off a critical decision, ask yourself, "what might I know in 10 days that I don't know now?" Over the years, I have definitely lost some ground when a team put too much energy into making a vendor, partner, or staff relationship work when in reality we all knew it was not working out. We saw the early warning signs but didn't act swiftly enough.

Maintaining a Dialogue

When thinking about the size of the team of people it took to get the Foundation to the point of the wristband campaign and then the team of people it required to maintain the success and help it continue to grow, it's easy to see how each person involved has been so talented and dedicated. Each member—past, present, future—represents our core values and the culture of the organization so well.

From the time the campaign originally launched, we definitely were an "all hands on deck" campaign. From interns to directors, we pulled together every development team member to talk about how the campaign would integrate into their daily work to figure out how much time they would have available to help with a variety of tasks. We did this all while maintaining our weekly development team meetings and working diligently to ensure that our other fundraising campaigns were still supported. It was necessary for all of our campaigns to succeed to meet the needs of our constituents, while we launched this new huge opportunity.

There were a ton of impromptu meetings taking place in offices up and down the hall whenever needed. I refer to these as "quick second" meetings because typically the person requesting the exchange would start by saying, "Do you have a quick second?" The flexibility of communication you get in an office setting is interesting to note as I wonder if we would have been as successful if we were a virtual team. Would we have been able to handle the amount of work and facilitate the necessary discussions? There is something to be said for spending time together and working through problems face-to-face. If I were going into the campaign all over again, I would require everyone to be in the office for key segments of the planning and encourage as much exchange as possible between various team members. This is because each con-versation led to something new or another question that needed to be answered. The open dia-logue resulted in solutions that could easily be implemented and communicated to the team with minimum lag time.

"Opportunity is in the person, not the job."
—Zig Ziglar

Although there were several people working on the campaign internally, each one had a designated role and played a specific part and there were always people being pulled into discussions from all over the country. While the Foundation team was all together in one office in Texas, our counterparts at

Nike were in Oregon. The point I want to make is that you should not assume that because you are a team of one or because your team might be spread out across the globe that a campaign of this magnitude is outside the realm of possibilities. It is really a question of scale. For an organization with an annual operating budget of $1,000,000, the creation of a campaign that generates $5,000,000 a year could have a tremendous impact but is something that, if simple enough, can be managed by a small and passionate team. Also, remember that not every campaign needs 20 people working on it. In the case of LIVESTRONG, we felt it was essential to engage every employee in this opportunity. For other campaigns we assigned duties accordingly and left campaign leadership to a few talented individuals. Simply put, there is not just one organizational chart or process that applies to every campaign.

> *"People who commit themselves to a goal have an impact on the lives of those around them. Enthusiasm and commitment are contagious."*
> —David Cottrell

A good rule of thumb is to create work groups that cut across departments and divisions and hold leaders accountable. And don't be afraid to limit new opportunities to your best and brightest. There have been a long line of organizations that have provided new and exciting opportunities to the top tier of their organization, both in for-profit and nonprofit organizations. One example is the launch of the Lexus brand. Toyota did not immediately send the cars to all 1600 of their dealers. They chose 81 of the very best dealers in the country. Perfection was required and they assembled a team that would buy into the vision and also help execute it accordingly. When you are planning to launch a new campaign or pilot a concept, do you feel compelled to share it equally among your chapters or organization? If so, that might not always be the best path. It definitely does not provide incentive for those groups or individuals that need to be doing better and it can set your program up for failure. Internally, be sure to include every department or position that could be even slightly impacted by the campaign. In the case of the LIVESTRONG campaign, we were dealing with a variety of issues so it was critical to not only involve the development team but to engage accounting, marketing and communications, technology, and operations. Every department was impacted by most decisions and needed to provide input on those decisions and the subsequent plans.

Also, keep in mind there should be some flexibility in that every team member will not be putting in the same amount of hours to a project or campaign as others. Some people only need to participate a few hours a week while others can find their jobs consumed with a campaign. I do not recommend equal distribution of work just for the sake of being fair. Tasks should go to the most qualified person. Team members whose jobs are closely tied to the success or failure of the campaign should be willing to step up in a large way when it comes time to activate a partnership.

★   ★   ★

Remember that organizations don't create change but that people make change happen. This is especially true when your mission is life or death. In other words, it is important to know who you are standing next to on the battlefield during a campaign. Learn about your team members. Ask essential questions including:

- How long have colleagues been with an organization?
- Where were they previously?
- What are they passionate about?
- What motivates them?
- How can you help them?

While growing as a team internally at the Foundation, everyone working on the wristband campaign also had a sense that we were part of a much larger Nike/Foundation team. Be sure your immediate team is open to the possibilities of being a part of something special and that they aren't intimidated or reluctant to get involved. Whenever opportunities are presented, a sense of urgency is important. Commit to people who you believe will bear fruit for the organization and your partners.

"Concentrate on doing a single task as simply as you can, execute it flawlessly, take care of your people and go home."
—USMC Maj. Davis

Your team will also determine how effectively you can mobilize those around you, your target audiences, and the general public. Integration internally is the first step, but that can set the tone for future involvement of others in the campaign. Getting people engaged and motivated to take action is not an easy task and there are potential roadblocks at every step of the way. Identifying those for your team and your audiences ahead of time can help expand support for the project.

Chapter 7

Strategies for Integrating and Mobilizing

Make everything yellow! Everything!

This was the rally cry of the LIVESTRONG campaign team. We wanted everyone, everywhere in yellow. We relied on each individual member of the various extended teams and partners to determine the best possible way to integrate the campaign into their already pre-scheduled activities. These activities included selling wristbands at events, engaging advocates at advocacy day (which later became Yellow Day on Capitol Hill), and direct marketing integration. Aside from the core team, we never told anyone how to paint their program yellow or exactly what the best method would be. I often refer to a quote from Paul Guitierrez, "The job itself wasn't creative...but our job was to *be* creative." We simply made the challenge to everyone— "how are you going to support the LIVESTRONG effort?"— and left the creativity, strategy, and tactics to the extended team. Our initial response presentation to Nike after we heard about the wristband idea demonstrated our willingness to engage everyone. Our presentation clearly stated that our focus was to mobilize the cancer community through our existing partners, events, advocates, and programs. We started with the smallest ideas and concepts, and grew each one into a full campaign module.

"Your courage is ultimately measured by how much it takes to discourage you."
—David Cottrell

While we at the Lance Armstrong Foundation (Foundation) were busy thinking about all of the resources at our disposal, Nike was also working to create the broadest reach possible for the LIVESTRONG wristband campaign. Nothing was off limits——whether it was traditional media, access to Nike athletes, connecting with Nike's entertainment influencers, digital on Nike.com and the creation of wearyellow.com, corporate executive peer-to-peer outreach by Phil Knight, the CEO of Nike, integration with Nike community affairs projects like NIKEGO, or retail presence at Niketown and select retail partners. We knew that we would have to access all of these segments if we were to be successful.

On Integrating: A Few Lessons Learned

Our team worked hard to think of every possible concern or issue that could arise during the campaign. No matter how hard you try, there will still be issues you encounter as your campaign progresses. Whether it's staffing, legal, accounting, or donor relations issues, it is hard to imagine the sheer number of topics and issues brought on by a campaign of this magnitude. These partnerships are a classic example of "you don't know what you don't know." I am hoping that while much of this book discusses the strategies and basic principles of cause-marketing and corporate-partnership programs, that some of the book also provides tactical support and education for your future campaign initiatives.

Starting Early with Accounting

Be sure you have strong finance and legal teams who are working diligently to ensure accurate reporting and proper stewardship of donor gifts. Prior to launching a corporate partnership program, identify a point person in accounting for development issues and develop a relationship with your legal counsel. Set time aside each month to talk through the headlines and evaluate current programs or complications from other public campaigns and discuss how your organization would approach a similar issue. Any time you spend now building that relationship will be a huge win later on when you are dealing with a specific campaign related to your organization.

Take the time early in the campaign to build the proper reports. Avoid anything that may damage your financial standings within the charity or donor communities. Also, learn and appreciate each department's needs and limitations. You will be better equipped to help each other when the time comes.

One debate that I hear continually at nonprofits is the timing of assigning a partnership or campaign its own account code for tracking purposes. Usually, the development team does not see a need to track each separate opportunity until it becomes a solid program that is actually revenue generating. Meanwhile, the accounting team takes the stance that by waiting until revenue is generated, the organization never truly captures all of the campaign-creation costs. They reason that any expenses incurred before the official signing of the contract would just go into the general cause-marketing budget and not be properly allocated. Identify the right time to assign the accounting code for your organization and follow the process diligently. In most cases, I recommend assigning the accounting code early in the conversations. Even though this sometimes causes some more work on the front end and you will learn a month later that the campaign is not launching or the partnership has fizzled, it's a good idea to be ready. This is much easier than trying to go back through your records in order to recode and identify charges and time that might have been associated with a campaign. Err on the side of optimism here and build an infrastructure that assumes you are going to get the green light and hit it out of the park, and then scale back if and when you need to.

When you are launching a campaign or beginning to discuss it internally, publish the accounting code quickly so that every person engaged in the process can track their expenses and time to the campaign. Just generating a response to a potential partner can involve video, presentations, and more. Be sure you understand your potential partner's preferred communication style and provide a relevant response or initial presentation. You will notice that some companies are very visual and enjoy the use of images while others tend to focus on facts and figures. Adjust your presentations accordingly. The solicitation of cause-marketing partnerships will require an initial investment by the charity and you need to track that accordingly.

> *"Lack of direction, not lack of time, is the problem. We all have twenty-four hour days."*
> —Zig Ziglar

When launching a cause-marketing program that involves a product or service, be sure to establish a 'complimentary item' policy early on with your accounting team. Every organization has key supporters that may normally receive premium items as stewardship or cultivation items. But, in the case of a campaign like the wristband campaign, I recommend making the decision early on that every item be paid for, including those that the charity distributes themselves.

Work with your accounting team and the rest of the organization to discover upcoming activities and constituent segments that should include items and then created a list of underwriting opportunities for donors and sponsors. This forced us to reach out to our donors, sponsors, and other partners to help us distribute wristbands to our advocates, cyclists, and donors. While it may seem hard to message early on that there will be no free items, it will be a nice opportunity for other organizations to feel intimately involved in the campaign and facilitate some really great conversations with donors that you can expand upon later. This is reason to keep your program very simple. It makes it easier to say "you have to pay."

Many campaigns fail before they get started because so much of the value is given away to the key audience through comps and other giveaways. If the program you have created is going to be a winner to the general public or a targeted audience you have selected, chances are those closest to you will not mind getting involved even if that means making a financial contribution. This decision can generate lots of money instead of freebies that you will be responsible for distributing, and as an added bonus, it will save time for the team. You will be able to quickly dismiss complimentary item requests and won't feel any pressure to hand out the products freely. The idea of purchasing the item should be made clear to everyone regardless of past involvement or number of connections. Set a clear policy everyone can adhere to and it will be understood and respected by your supporters.

Embracing New Avenues with Grantees

The LIVESTRONG campaign was also the first time the fundraising team fully integrated with our grantees in a fundraising capacity. Previously, the programs team maintained all programmatic relationships and had not involved them in fundraising efforts. Our development team knew from direct marketing research that often times the people that an organization serves can become its largest base of support. Prior to the wristband campaign, we had not tapped into this resource.

We were very sensitive to the concern of cannibalizing our grantees' donor base but equally concerned with complicating the wristband message with joint fundraising messaging. Once we came up with a call to action for the grantee audience, we reached out. The messaging worked and the campaign was easy to engage with. The orders started pouring in and the grantees saw an opportunity to be a part of something larger. All of the organizations realized that by helping to support the wristband campaign, the entire cancer community would be positively impacted. And to further incentivize our grantee partners, we developed programs so that the grantees that were most successful with their wristband sales would qualify for prizes and other benefits. Of course every new component of the campaign added some logistical challenges, but their grassroots support was worth the time and energy and was essential to the campaign.

Combining Marketing Platforms Effectively

When you are launching a new marketing or cause-marketing campaign, it is important to remember that not every communication channel will react the same way. I have seen occasions when a mass market tagline or advertising campaign was implemented in a direct response campaign. The message was not tailored enough for the audience and the message did not resonate with donors and overall response rates were much lower than normal. If you end up making a few of these types of integrations each year, it can affect the overall programs results and jeopardize those efforts.

In regards to direct response, donors respond best to a very clear and concise call to action, which is to donate. By trying to integrate a "share your story concept" or "click this link to generate a donation by a partnering company," you run the risk of losing the donor permanently. Good marketing ideas can suffer if the right channel and audience is not determined early on. Do not be overly eager to integrate concepts just for the sake of integration. Be sure it truly will make a positive difference for the organization.

There were instances of this during the wristband campaign and it was interesting to see how in so many ways the LIVESTRONG wristband had positively impacted our organization but it reminded us that it wasn't going to make everything magically easier. We still needed to apply best practices, pilot our ideas, and work hard to further the cause. It would not come easy because everyone suddenly knew our name.

We learned that not every campaign concept should be launched or used organization wide. The execution of the campaign should be different depending on the medium and the audience. Get expert advice and then trust those you have hired to give you good recommendations. Make integration decisions as a team and apply all previous lessons learned.

Integrating Diverse Digital Real Estate Assets

The LIVESTRONG campaign would require an increase in the organization's online presence. At the time, the main web site was www.laf.org. However, the Foundation maintained a number of web sites that were being marketed to different audiences at any given time such as a site for grantees to apply for funding or cycling event participants to get information about upcoming events. We had to find a way to integrate the LIVESTRONG wristband campaign messages into each of these digital assets. Other sites that we either managed internally or had access to but hadn't leveraged prior to the campaign included LIVESTRONG.org and tourofhope.com. LIVESTRONG.org had just launched as the online resource center for cancer survivors. Tourofhope.com was a web site managed by our pharmaceutical partner. It had been created two years earlier to support a coast-to-coast tour of cyclists with a cancer connection. On the site, people were asked to sign a cancer promise which encouraged clinical trial participation. When the wristband campaign was developed, we worked with the site owner to create an opportunity for people to get a wristband in exchange for signing the cancer promise. It allowed us to integrate the wristband into an already successful partner program and gave a clear call to action for the audience of that site. In addition, Lance's cycling team was preparing to launch Paceline. com in the spring of 2004. Lance's agent and the web site team promised to dedicate web site real estate to promoting the bands to their members and fans.

Don't just think about your organization's main web site. Be sure to include a full list of assets including sites you own and manage, third-party sites, partner sites, and more. Had Twitter and Facebook been as widespread as they are now, I am sure we would have integrated those into our digital planning as well.

Keeping Ahead in Advocacy Efforts

Through the years, the Foundation and Lance had begun to develop relationships with both state and national government policymakers. Our government outreach had been steadily growing in the years prior to the campaign. These advocacy efforts were delivering results. We were asking for an increased focus on quality-of-life issues after a diagnosis and working to make cancer a national priority.

When our LIVESTRONG efforts began, we immediately looked to the government-relations team to support the campaign. We agreed to find a sponsor to underwrite the distribution of wristbands to every member of Congress and hand-delivered the bands using our advocates. Our day on the hill transformed into LIVESTRONG Day and attendance steadily increased each year. The policymakers were pleased to be involved with a charity that was on the front page of most major magazines and newspapers and it did wonders for gaining attention for the cause. We were pleased when many of the election candidates were spotted wearing wristbands and

"It's risky out on the limb, but that's where all the fruit is."
—Robin Sharma

we continued to utilize our notoriety to host Presidential debates and get commitments from candidates that cancer was a priority. We actively shared this information with our constituents and the program has continued to net results and make an impact.

Acknowledging Other Special Concerns

When thinking through execution in campaigns, especially larger ones, be aware of issues that might not normally come up in other typical courses of business. In some cases you may encounter new situations in the fields of customs, fraud, and manufacturing.

If dealing with overseas manufacturing, find a partner with international experience to help you handle customs issues. You can find specialized legal teams to help with fraud issues. You will find it necessary to know more than you ever wanted to about prosecution of fraud or similar concerns. Be prepared to learn more than you ever wanted to know about manufacturing and specific contents of items you are using for the promotion. Be aware of these types of issues that need to be addressed and find the resources that can help alleviate the burden on the team. If it can be handled efficiently and quickly do it and move on, but if it is going to become an ongoing need, allocate the proper resources and don't distract the core team from their mission. Investigate to find out who and what you need to know to make informed and intelligent decisions.

Depending on your campaign, you may be dealing with a product that is not already distributed. You may end up dealing with fraud, trademark infringement, manufacturing, and customs issues that can lead to weeks of backorders when your campaign is going strong. Take every opportunity to exceed customer expectations and provide high quality service. Each interaction with your organization should be meaningful and people should leave the interaction with a feeling that you were responsive to their needs—no matter how small. Be extremely customer focused just as you expect the same from your programs team. It is also an opportunity to begin a long-term relationship with each campaign participant.

Keeping Your Plan Simple but Effective

The Foundation was able to amass a large grassroots network with other grant organizations, support groups, and more. This was a significant asset we brought to the LIVESTRONG wristband campaign and a key focus for us winning partnership opportunities with Nike. But coordinating a grassroots network does not come easily. It takes considerable effort, project management skills, and diligence on everyone's part.

We used several tools to help us effectively mobilize the network. One tool that we used was a simple spreadsheet that had four columns. The column headings included Project Name, Person Responsible, Action Item, and Wristband Goal. The spreadsheet was populated based on our promise to Nike. We had made estimates for each wristband distribution channel based on the data we had available. The spreadsheet also included milestones such as logistics meetings and key decisions that needed to be made that would warrant team discussions. The document evolved throughout the campaign and at one point we added an entire section for Nike employee integration opportunities. An example of that outreach included making arrangements for Nike employees to distribute wristbands at local hospitals and cancer centers in Portland. This hands-on experience added value to Nike and the campaign but it was important that we tracked the opportunity and could verify its completion.

> *"I am a great believer in luck. The harder I work the more I have of it."*
> —Thomas Jefferson

On Mobilizing: A Few Lessons Learned

What does it mean to mobilize someone or a group of people? Getting people to move or take action is sometimes enough. But for the wristband campaign, we needed people not only to conduct outreach or buy a band, but for those closest to us we needed them to engage with us. Help us understand how they could contribute in a meaningful way to the campaign and what support or resources we would need to provide.

Designating Points of Contact

Watch out what you wish for. We had discussed the campaign with so many groups and organizations that when the time came to consider each opportunity and determine a course of action it was hard to keep up. With so many people working on the LIVESTRONG campaign, it was easy for an opportunity to get lost in the shuffle. Our champions at Nike wanted to be sure that if another corporate partner of the Foundation was interested in participating in the campaign, they would be given all of the information available in order to activate and support our efforts. And they wanted to ensure the vision for the project was clearly communicated. The team prepared all of the messaging and collateral in order to activate all companies interested in participating in the campaign. The companies that reached out to the Foundation appreciated the ability to network and work alongside Nike. Nike enjoyed helping us leverage each opportunity. Individual and non-wristband corporate opportunities were addressed by the appropriate staff or volunteers at the Foundation. Volunteers worked with the Director of Volunteers, and event participants talked directly with the event managers. Media contacts maintained their relationship with our marketing and communication department contacts. Because the campaign was so big, there was no physical way for one person to be the point of contact for everyone.

I have seen many groups that have attempted to designate one person to read every piece of collateral or review every use of the logo. It never works. To really achieve the greatness you are hoping for in a large campaign, you need to be more flexible. Ask yourself if the system you are currently using adds value to the campaign in the long run. Decide what tools and resources you need to implement in order to remove the gatekeeper mentality that can besiege campaigns. What kind of training needs to take place with your teams—both internal and external—so they are equipped and empowered to do their jobs and be effective extensions of the core team?

For example, at the time of LIVESTRONG's launch, we had several corporate partners that were supporting the Foundation either through cause-marketing campaigns, event sponsorship, or program underwriting and grants. We saw this group of companies as being able to help mobilize our supporters. Nike encouraged their involvement. They were eager to share the campaign resources including tools, branding, and publicity. It was clear that this was not about one sponsor trying to make a difference, but rather one partner that was leading others in a group effort of improving the lives of cancer survivors everywhere. Our partners were eager to work with a company like Nike and it elevated our conversations with every partner across the board.

Showcasing Your Benefits

Do not give away everything for nothing. Be selective with which partners and which campaigns you utilize every possible resource and asset. The commitment and scale of the campaign will help determine the appropriate charity efforts. Be specific about the partnership placement and sponsorship benefits you provide because the commitment from both sides needs to be mutually as deep and meaningful. Knowing when to pull out all the stops and when to reserve benefits for partners that have not yet materialized is an important lesson and a tricky thing to balance. With every relationship we entered, the Foundation spent a fair amount of time ensuring that the benefits we promised and the activation ideas we presented were plausible for us. We did not promise things like national media because we had no way of delivering on that promise or controlling the outcome. We worked together to uncover additional leveraging opportunities. We were honest and transparent about our assets and then it was the job of the combined team to examine everything and find the diamonds in the rough.

Take Advantage of the Urgency

When looking back at my notes from the early days of our campaign, I am struck with the speed at which we pulled so many pieces of the LIVESTRONG campaign together. Nike presented the concept at the end of January 2004 and we had about three to four weeks to come up with a plan. We responded with a presentation and video in March.

> "Opportunities multiply as they are seized."
> —John Wicker

The first wristband was publicly distributed in mid-April at the Lance Armstrong Foundation Gala in Austin, Texas. Lance rode and won his sixth Tour de France in July of that same year. From the initial idea presentation to the launch of the campaign, it was less than four months time. When an opportunity arises and the path toward its goals is right, people will rally around it and make it happen. There will be a burning desire to make the impossible possible. Your team and those impacted by your cause will help you move mountains.

*   *   *

When reviewing our approaches from 2004, I know there are ways in which we could have taken our integration and mobilization steps further if we had further engaged each group with which we were involved. For instance, let's take another look at the grantee outreach strategy discussed earlier in the chapter. Our team at the Foundation created the outreach plan and then communicated it to the grantees. Do not forget to engage your group of core constituents in the development of the plan instead of simply reaching out once it had been decided—this is a key opportunity to connect with your audience and make sure the program resonates with those you serve. Do not handle the mobilization as outreach instead of engagement—it will be a mistake you will regret.

Organizations with national offices and chapters are forced to engage each other frequently for a variety of needs and problems. This is where that structure can serve as an asset for a campaign. Organizations using that model may be more comfortable with massive engagement at every stage of the process and could use this skill effectively during the creation of a campaign. And, as referenced in Chapter 1, timing is everything. Determining at what stages of development and planning you should involve others is a key decision point. When are you currently engaging difference segments of your audience and is there room for improvement? Identify the key points in the planning where people can have a maximum impact and return on investment of their time and energy.

Using tools like the spreadsheet noted here is one way to track how effectively you are engaging other people and organizations in the campaign. Prior to launch, be sure to think about how you will measure success, how you will gather those metrics and generate a baseline so you are aware of where you are starting from. Building in feedback systems is also helpful so that instead of reflecting on solid insights after the campaign has already been completed, you can course correct along the way.

Chapter 8

Creating Feedback Mechanisms

*Capturing Information, Assessing Your Work,
and Considering the Future*

O rganizations have an obligation on the front
end of campaigns to create mechanisms to
capture data that may have a long–term
impact on the organization. These capturing systems
and infrastructure are necessary to leverage an organization's investment in the program or campaign. In
hindsight, the Lance Armstrong Foundation (Foundation) missed a large opportunity to capture information
on a majority of wristband purchasers. It was difficult
to implement an efficient and non–disruptive acquisition program in retail outlets. Be sure you identify and
communicate a compelling reason for people to engage

with the Foundation beyond just the cause-marketing purchase. Implementing a system like this for the wristband campaign would have been helpful. As Doug Ulman reflected, "Our number-one mistake was not capturing people during the campaign."

In fact, the only contact information captured in the Foundation databases was from online purchasers. This totaled about 1 million names and email addresses. This was a far cry from the more than 70 million wristbands distributed. The Foundation has since implemented mechanisms to learn more about the people that purchased wristbands through surveys and the "Share Your Story" campaign. But, the efforts to recover the information not captured at that critical moment in time have not even come close to capturing the actual number of people invested in the cause given the success of the wristband.

Opportunities for Feedback

Along with not capturing people as they purchased a wristband, another missed opportunity was not building feedback mechanisms into the campaign. The idea of gathering feedback from participants and others engaged in the LIVESTRONG wristband campaign was not a priority but should have been. We were diligent about asking for advice prior to making a decision. However, once a decision had been made, we would move forward at full speed and tend to consider the conversation complete, which was not the case. It is just as important to touch base with the people impacted by your decision and make additional revisions and seek constant improvements. You will receive the occasional comment or call that will cause you to pause and make minor adjustments but this is very reactionary. Proactively establish clear feedback loops. This applies for both feedback from external or outside audiences as well as from your own team members. You should be able to reflect back on the campaign and recall times when you gathered the team after a major deliverable was completed and asked the questions "how did that go?" or "what should we have done differently?"

We were all learning at every step of the process within the campaign. Many small mistakes or speed bumps can be avoided by getting additional feedback throughout the process. It would have been helpful to host more regular debrief meetings and determine actionable changes throughout the campaign. We could have also used online surveying tools to publish a survey to ask about the purchasing process or an individual's LIVESTRONG experience. It would have been great to know if we had provided all of the resources necessary to fully activate our grassroots network. Once we launched the partner web site, we really did not follow up and ask questions of groups on both ends of the usage spectrum. I believe we could have gained a lot of information if we had identified partners that chose not to engage with the campaign and asked them why or gave them a forum to explain their decisions. And, on the other side of the spectrum, it would have been wonderful to speak directly with those organizations that were actively using the resources we had provided and ask what else would be helpful or what tools have been the most effective in their experiences.

Feedback does not have to be complicated. It can be as simple as picking up the phone or creating a five-minute survey that can be answered online. We did do some research regarding the why behind people's purchase of the band but we didn't ask about the campaign itself and what resonated or didn't resonate. There are outbound call centers, surveying and research companies, and countless resources online that are focused on helping an organization capture meaningful feedback. Be sure to include this as an action item on your campaign project plan and set time aside to analyze the results. And be sure to do it when you can still utilize the information and insights to improve the program. When feedback-gathering systems are in place, they provide people with a forum to discuss ideas and insights. And you can learn from recent experiences. Otherwise, knowledge share is limited and not scalable. The time spent on reflection should be built into campaign project plans. It should also be included in account management of partnerships, regardless of size. Look at the impact of a strong Yelp. com score for a restaurant, the impact of a Rotten Tomato score on a movie's box office sales, or the helpfulness of recommendations on LinkedIn when applying for a job. Since the campaign in 2004, there has been a huge boom in user-generated content web sites including review and feedback sites. Your mission is more critical than the decision of where to eat or what movie to see. So, be sure you are not just gathering feedback but also make some feedback opportunities very public and share the results with others. If they can see that someone was genuinely impressed with your customer service or that an existing partner is impressed with your team, they can better understand you and it can serve to motivate them to want to get involved.

> *"Someone to tell it to is one of the fundamental needs of human beings."*
> —Miles Franklin

We often gathered around the conference table at the Foundation offices and had long conversations about operational concerns that should be addressed. These things are important and should not be overlooked because the devil can be in the details. But it is important to find the time to talk about whether or not you reached your objectives for the campaign and why you think you either made the goals or missed them. Use the times you gather the entire team to think big. Don't squander this time thinking about things like email–subject–line tweaks or other tiny details. Be willing to take some conversations offline if they affect a few or don't directly impact the team's ability to execute the plan and achieve the larger goals. Team debrief time should be spent evaluating the key drivers that impacted the success or mission of the team. Key drivers can include the types of groups you engaged, the technology ease of use, or the motivation of your closest mission ambassadors and whether or not it was effective overall. These key drivers are the levers that you can adjust to help ensure you reach your goal the next time around. It is up to the individuals on the team to remember the details of their role and how they can make continued improvements.

To this point, debrief meetings are also not a time to be assessing staff or team changes. I think one of the biggest mistakes a leader can make is not allowing someone to learn from their failure and do it better next time. Many times people end up replacing team members for any number of reasons and end up losing those lessons learned within the organization. Taking this path results in the same mistakes potentially being made the second time around. There is a motto that I like to refer to after each time I feel a sense of failure with a particular project or task and that is "Every great success follows a great failure." If you think about it, this thought can provide a sense of hope when you think your recent shortcomings will potentially hinder you long term but also makes you realize that you aren't taking enough risks if you don't experience failure at some point in the process. And, I am more anxious to get those failures out of the way so I can move on to bigger and better things. This does not mean that I am a fan of letting people make the same mistakes twice or that sometimes a staffing change is required for the good of the team and the larger organization. This is simply a word of caution about why you are making that decision and not immediately connecting a staff change with a campaign that does reach its goals.

It is interesting to think about what would change with regular campaign evaluation discussions. How would the conversation affect the direction of the campaign? Since the campaign, new technologies have made it possible to integrate data capture into the purchase process. These new updates may be relevant during your campaign and you should look for integration opportunities. Had these systems been available at the time of the campaign, we would have had the opportunity to acquire purchaser data without causing a delay at check out or creating a high barrier to entry for the customers. If you have feedback loops developed and you are actively asking improvement questions the entire time during the campaign, you will recognize an opportunity to make a change. Once you know there is a problem you can find a solution!

Using Metrics

Metrics are also an important piece of feedback on your progress and success. The overarching success metric was to sell five million wristbands. That is what we were all working toward. Once that was completed we knew we had achieved our goal. We did not have a campaign dashboard or other tool to measure the key drivers or other desired outcomes from the campaign and those results were delivered very anecdotally. This was unfortunate because it didn't allow us to capture all of the intangibles of the campaign. It also didn't provide us with a historical view of when the tipping point occurred or when a certain audience segment became engaged. There was not real breakout of information. It was simply the number of bands sold and the number that remained.

At the Foundation, we were measuring quite a few logistics functions such as backorder time, number of wristbands sold in a day (which hit 100,000 the day we were on Oprah!), and number of media impressions. It would have been helpful to monitor the growth in our database, the increase in registration rates for our volunteer, advocacy, or events programs, and the number of incoming calls and emails to our programs department of people needing cancer support and patient navigation as well. I urge you to create a report dashboard that should monitor five or six measurements. You might originally come up with a list of 20 key drivers to measure, but filter these down to the ones that matter most. What will the number tell you? Will the number drive change if it is high or low? Does it impact the long term for the organization? Is it something that can be shared with your partners so they can see how their involvement in your mission was helpful?

A dashboard report will also help consolidate the massive number of individual metrics being measured by various individuals and departments within the organization. Specific to the LIVESTRONG wristband campaign we found ourselves in a situation where different departments and partners were measuring their own targets. For example, the online resource center team was watching the usage rates on the web site, whereas our technology team, was monitoring the store analytics. The finance team were tracking our revenue and expenses. A central point of coordination and metrics monitoring would have been a tremendous gift for the Foundation and could have been used to help guide future campaigns and partnerships. It would have also provided more data to analyze regarding the how and

> *"When something is missing in your life, it usually turns out to be someone."*
> —Robert Brault

why the LIVESTRONG wristband campaign was successful. This consolidated dashboard would provide a high-level picture of how the campaign was doing but also provide relevant and actionable data points to the various members of the team.

I think if we had worked to establish this up front we would have caught the fact that we were missing key information and meaningful metrics. We would have identified those gaps and would have made the program that much more successful for the Foundation over the long term. Build this for your organization today so you are ready to launch the campaign and monitor your success instead of waiting and determining it isn't a must do so it falls to the bottom of your to-do list.

Knowing Your Priorities

Speaking of your to-do list, you may propose various campaign components, like data capture, but they do not register with the partner or aren't made a priority. Be sure you are seeking opportunities for how the program can impact your organization both short and long term and share those opportunities with your partner pre-launch. You may receive some push back to these requests and it will be important to keep the simplicity of the campaign in mind. Determine when it is appropriate to trust your partner's instincts but also do not be afraid to push back. The long-term vision for these programs is not just to have a successful cause-marketing campaign but to create lasting change. Your partners will know this but typically they will have

mechanisms in place to expand the customer relationship and won't understand your urge to capture the
customers. Your organization will have one real chance
of engaging with the consumer and capturing them in
a way that will begin a dialogue. When you are creating a true partnership, be sure both partners are aware
of the factors that are most important to each other.
Concern about not capturing your supporters is not
new for nonprofit organizations. Every time a charity
hosts a gala or radio-thon, hundreds of donors attend
or participate and those names are never captured. For
galas, organizations will collect the name of the table
purchasers but not the name of their guests. Then what
happens is the guest decides to purchase the largest live
auction item or makes a cash donation before they
leave for the evening. That donor is lost. You can try
to go back after the fact and track down the table they
were sitting at, reach out to the table purchasers and
so on, but rarely does that provide results. In regard to
the LIVESTRONG wristband campaign and all other
opportunities for engagement, build in the opportunity
to capture these motivated and inspired people. You
need to have the systems in place to capture names—
whether that is 10 people at a gala table or 75 million
people wearing wristbands and consider the lifetime
value of a donor instead of the value of the one-time
cause-marketing participation.

Social Media, Loyalty, and Growth

Doug Ulman and the team at LIVESTRONG have
been using social media since 2005 as a way to engage

and capture as many supporters as possible. Doug refers to it as the next phase of the wristband campaign. Social media has allowed LIVESTRONG to play an active part in people's daily lives. Through a host of social media venues including staff Twitter accounts, an active Facebook community, and a LIVESTRONG YouTube channel they are part of people's daily experiences. In 2004, we began exploring new business initiatives and potential strategies for the Foundation moving forward. Randall and I discussed the benefits of finding ways to integrate the Lance Armstrong Foundation into the existing path of our constituents instead of expecting them to come to us. We would discuss concepts that would potentially allow us to become entangled in people's daily routines. We felt strongly that this was the way to grow LIVESTRONG. It would support it as a lasting brand and force in the world and would not require those we serve to make all of the effort. Now, social media tools make this concept a reality in a way that's effective and efficient. "If you build it they will come" is not always true. Organizations must provide solutions and go to their people to truly make a difference. Ask yourself, "Am I going to my constituents or expecting them to come to me?" LIVESTRONG has dedicated a team of people to supporting and sustaining its digital presence. It has a strategy that involves both existing technologies as well as testing those that might become a part of society in the future. These relationships with key technology companies and advisors allow LIVESTRONG to stay current while monitoring the tools that are most impactful for the organization in both awareness and fundraising.

And, while the Foundation has dedicated staff to social media efforts, it has also embraced the concept of allowing staff and other volunteers to readily identify themselves as such online. This creates multiple connections with the organization for the average LIVESTRONG advocates and supporters. For example, I follow Doug Ulman on Twitter and I also follow several other staff members and volunteers. On Facebook, I am friends with the official LIVESTRONG page but also am friends with LIVESTRONG advocates in a variety of states that regularly share LIVESTRONG messages and the importance of LIVESTRONG in their lives. This demonstrates the power of using social media to communicate and to capture your supporters, it should be noted that Doug Ulman is the number one non-celebrity on Twitter according to number of followers. He has more than one million followers to date.

> "Sometimes you have to get to know someone really well to realize you're really strangers."
> —Mary Tyler Moore

*   *   *

Not everyone that wore a wristband was destined to become a loyal LIVESTRONG advocate or lifetime supporter. Some people simply wore the band because of fashion and never planned on taking another action to benefit the cause. You should determine the breakdown of organization loyalists that would be willing to take further action for the cause and those that are interested but will not actively engage with you until directly impacted by the cause. Your job is to become intimately involved with the loyal group as quickly as possible, and to be ready when the rest of your database comes knocking on your door.

> *"Treasure your relationships, not your possessions."*
> —Anthony J. D'Angelo

Based on the unfortunate prevalence of cancer, we knew it was probably just a matter of time until many of these wristband supporters would reach out to us for help and we wanted to be ready. When you start breaking your audiences into categories, be sure to be aware of these two very distinct audience groups. They will engage differently with your organization. Someone in the inactive group can change into more of an active, loyal constituent instantly, so be prepared. Dedicate time to thinking about the constituent's lifecycle with the organization or campaign. Ask yourself the following questions:

- Has our engagement strategy been built so that people can get involved whenever the time is right for them?
- Do we know if people move between groups and how do we know when that is happening? Is there anything we could or should do about it?
- Are we talking differently to our most loyal supporters?
- Do we know the names of our most dedicated of that 20 percent group? Have we recently asked them for feedback or insights?
- When was the last time we engaged them beyond online exchanges?

Starting with those you serve and thinking about your partners, your staff, and your extended network, have you defined a vision for how each of these groups will engage with your organization in the future? Having an idea of where you are headed and what it looks like when you achieve success can help you attract others that want to be a part of that vision. Knowing your story and how you came to be up to this point is important. You can use the tools here to share that message and to get feedback on its effectiveness for those you serve and hope to attract to the cause, and ultimately, your organization.

Attracting Nike and engaging our network in the wristband campaign would not have been as easy if the team at Nike had not helped paint the vision of a world covered in yellow. From the last image in their presentation, which was the Statue of Liberty wearing a wristband, to their storytelling about how the color yellow can impact people's lives in a tangible way providing hope and inspiration, they helped us see the vision of what we could become and what the cancer community could achieve if it united and made people pay attention to the cause.

Chapter 9

What It Takes to Be a Visionary

The cancer community has been blessed with amazing visionaries. Two of those are Lance Armstrong and our Nike representative. Lance did not originally envision an organization that would bring together the 28 million cancer survivors in the United States. He started the Lance Armstrong Foundation (Foundation) based on a statement from his doctor about an obligation of the cured. He didn't know exactly how this would manifest itself, but rather that if he could impact one other person and their survivorship journey he had done something to better the cancer community. Partnering that desire to help with the vision of scope and scale of Nike was a winning combination.

In regard to the wristband specifically, one person served as the catalyst for bringing all of the pieces together to create the cause-marketing campaign that changed the cancer community. I often reflect on the night in 2003 when our Nike contact and I were having a conversation at the welcome dinner of the annual Foundation's Golf Tournament. We were at a board member's home and discussing a variety of ideas, event concepts, and new program initiatives. It was at that dinner that the power of the color yellow was first mentioned to me. We had a conversation about what the color yellow meant to me and what I thought it meant to the cancer survivorship population. The vision had been born. Scott, our Nike contact felt the color yellow had the potential to be the thing that could galvanize more than just the cancer community. It could possibly bring together all people that believe in the idea of overcoming the odds and fighting like hell. The question that remained was how to package it in a way that made it relevant and accessible. Our Nike champion worked tirelessly to build momentum and support for this idea at Nike and rallied the best and brightest to help him turn this intangible concept into something we could each have a piece of.

One person inspired this idea of the color yellow and embodies the spirit of LIVESTRONG—a young athlete named John Brennan. John's sister had heard a Nike representative speak at her school. She asked the speaker for something of Lance's to give to her older brother. She explained that during his freshman year in college John was diagnosed with cancer and had lost his leg to it. They gave her a signed yellow jersey to present to John. John was overwhelmed by the gift and asked his mother what he should do with such a gift. His mom said, "If it makes you feel good, wear it!" After John returned home from the hospital, he changed into the jersey and came bounding down the stairs. He hit the bottom of the stairs with his fists in the air and yelled "I feel so empowered in this jersey!" His mom wrote to Nike and told them the story. Our Nike champion read the note and made the connection. Yellow equals empowerment.

"Vision without action is a dream. Action without vision is simply passing the time. Action with vision is making a positive difference."
—Joel Barker

Personally, I felt the power of the wristband as it related to my mother and her battle with breast cancer. Thankfully, she fought breast cancer successfully and was my original motivation to get involved in the cause. While I had never thought about my mom as a fighter before 1997—the year she was diagnosed—I saw a whole new side to her. Even before she knew about Lance or the Foundation, she embodied the spirit of the organization. At the moment of diagnosis, she was determined to fight with every ounce of her being. She was not willing to settle for the initial diagnosis or treatment recommendations. She wanted to make sure she was equipping herself with the best information and updated treatment options. She always had a positive attitude and was an inspiration to me throughout her year-long battle with the disease. I had never been able to make this spirit or sense of determination tangible until the baptism of my first son. I had given birth to Carter Edward in late April 2004, just following the initial launch of the wristband at the Lance Armstrong Foundation Gala. At the baptism in May, the priest asked the grandparents to make the sign of the cross on the baby's forehead. I watched my mother, standing in her beautiful white dress reach out with a bright yellow wristband on her arm and she was smiling from ear to ear. It was a reminder that I was lucky she was here to celebrate this joyous occasion with our family. I knew that she felt a sense of empowerment and pride to be wearing the LIVESTRONG wristband as a symbol of her fight but more importantly as an example to others that you can be diagnosed and still LIVESTRONG.

Sharing Your Story

People remember stories—not facts. I doubt that anyone will ever forget the story of John Brennan once they have heard it. There is no better way to motivate others than to tell them stories. You must provide stories that stir their hearts and also make it easy for people to share them with others. Stories help make your vision tangible and seem within reach. Stories of survivorship, triumph, and empowerment inspired the wristband campaign. What is your story?

Think about the stories you know of that embody what you are trying to accomplish. Are there glimpses that you have caught that give you an idea of what you want your organization to be and how it will serve others? Consider the stories you share with others. What stories do you share and what is the message that they communicate? Work to identify stories about meaningful partnerships and the work that you are doing together. This will send a clear message to incoming partners about how you work with those interested in your organization and cause and what they might be able to expect if they chose to do the same. Sit for a moment and contemplate what stories you will tell people about the organization after you are gone. What will you remember years from now that will immediately conjure up positive emotions and a desire to take action?

Early on at the Foundation, once we had decided to focus on cancer survivorship which we determined began at the moment a person is diagnosed and includes the patient and their loved ones—we knew the approximate size of our constituent base. We included the statistics on every presentation and video. We had charts and graphs that explained how the group would grow and change based on inputs such as diagnosis rates, survival rates, and average number of caregivers per diagnosis. It wasn't until the wristband that we could clearly convey how pervasive our constituent base was. We had known for a long time that the cancer community was widely dispersed and that at any given moment you were surrounded by people that had been directly impacted by the disease. We wanted to serve each of these individuals. We wanted to help the organizations that were currently providing services or conducting research that one day might make a difference. It seemed unfathomable that we would be able to actually tag each one of these people and have a clear way to identify them. But that is exactly what happened. Once the wristband became popular, everyone could see the size and scope of the cancer community in a very visible and tangible way. This included companies that would distribute wristbands internally or host Wear Yellow Day and register on our web site. We were able to identify the people and organizations and it was up to us to figure out how to engage them and supply the solutions to the issues and challenges they were faced with. The willingness of the cancer community and others to outwardly show their concern for our cause was a game changer for the Foundation. We were no longer relying on research statistics to tell our story.

Other organizations have worked to create similar tangible manifestations of support for their cause such as Wear Red Day for heart disease or making October pink for breast cancer awareness. When you are creating these types of campaigns, consider how third-party audiences will react or interpret the actions people are taking. Try to develop programs that will make it obvious to others that this cause is important. Another model to consider here is the world of politics. We can learn a lot from how those organizations engage and mobilize their support base and make it visible so that it will attract others to get involved. Whether support comes via Facebook group memberships, images on someone's Twitter account, bumper stickers on cars, yard signs, or by a willingness to invite others to a house party—political campaigns include multiple options for very visible

> *"A vision is not a mission. To state that an organization has a mission is to state its purpose, not its direction."*
> —Burt Nanus

shows of support. Apply the lessons you learn from studying those campaigns to your own efforts. Take the best of every program and create a cause-marketing program within your organization that is set up for success. And once it has launched, make sure and help people see your vision in action.

Sometimes you will be inspired by the opportunity to see your audience in action. But it will raise additional questions. You will ask about their motivation or connection to the cause or what their future plans are regarding engaging with your organization. I would like to offer a word of caution for everyone. While I am a fan of feedback through a variety of mechanisms, I think formal research studies also have a time and a place but should always include careful consideration. The wristband had really taken off and millions of people were wearing it. You couldn't go outside without seeing dozens of them. It was obvious that the Foundation was onto something, but it was hard to explain why exactly it was achieving such success.

The Foundation conducted various surveys to learn more about why people were wearing the band or how they were connected to the cause. Review of the data collected revealed that the Foundation already knew why people wanted to be a part of the campaign. We knew the cancer community. This is not to say that marketing research shouldn't be considered a valuable tool, but be sure you understand the end goal of the results. What questions are you trying to answer and what will you do with the information once you have it. Surveys can be useful tools and really help you understand your audience better and avoid pitfalls, but the questions you ask are paramount.

Communicating Your Vision

Knowing your audience will help you to more effectively communicate your vision. Everyone should have a vision for themselves and the organization they represent. This is very important and can drive every future choice you make. You can decide today to be different in five years or be exactly the same. Once you know where you want to end up, determine the steps you need to take to make that your reality.

One of the best ways to inspire a vision for you and your organization is to spend time with the people you want to impact. Watch, learn, listen, read—anything you can do to grasp a full picture of the situation. The Foundation was blessed with cancer survivors who readily spoke about their experiences. People everywhere approached Lance to say thank you and to share their stories. The team members were impacted by their own cancer experiences and that shaped our vision for partnerships, programs, and the services that we offered. When developing the LIVESTRONG online resource center, months were spent understanding and getting to know our constituents. That is where the name LIVESTRONG came from—countless conversations which resulted in a desire for unprecedented access and insights. How much time do you spend with those you serve? Spending time with people passionate about your cause also provides new stories of inspiration which are necessary to really rally people toward a vision. Michelangelo was once asked how he sculpted David, his marble masterpiece, to which he replied: "I saw David through the stone, and

I simply chipped away at everything that was not David." Get rid of things that don't fit!

I have had the privilege of working with a few people in my career who are masters of shedding the excess. They are relentless about getting rid of that which doesn't belong. One planning meeting with our executive leadership team was kicked off with a simple but thought provoking question. It was, "What should we stop doing?" Typically these meetings were filled with discussion after discussion about what to add to the organization. This new take on the conversation delivered great results and forced each of us to be more diligent about taking programs or campaigns for granted and being sure everything was relevant. And, the relevance of a project could change over time. Look at existing and proposed programs and partnerships. What doesn't fit? What should you think about phasing out? This mental exercise will help you bring up the tough topics and allow the team to make critical decisions related to removing things that are blocking or slowing down progress.

> "You are always only one choice away from changing your life."
>
> —Mary Blochowiak

You can expand on this exercise by taking an inventory of your time—how you currently spend it and how you would like to spend it. The end goal is to help you realize that you can make time for those things you deem most important. Start by writing your major time categories on the left hand side of the paper. For example, when I was the Director of

Development my list would have included things like human resources, event development, corporate relations, agreement facilitation, and executive-level reporting. Now, on the right side of the same piece of paper, write down the ways you would like to spend your time or where you think your time would be best spent. My list would have included some of the things on the left but also things like one-on-one time with key partners, strategic planning conversations, celebrating more achievements of the team, meaningful interactions with our constituents, and more. The next step, and the most critical in the exercise, is to remove the things from the left side that are not on the right. You just made time. Take that time and apply it to the things from the right side of the paper that you aren't currently doing. There is no reason for you not to be able to accomplish these things. I had a few "a-ha" moments throughout this process when I recently conducted the exercise for myself. Every time I am about to do something that was crossed off my list, I question the decision. I try to imagine using the time for something on the other side of the page. I ask myself if I would be better served to use that time catching up with an old client or spending time with my family.

How do you currently spend your time? Is that list different than the list of how you would like to spend your time or where you feel you should be spending your time? What is different between the two lists? Are there things you can remove and replace? Are you leveraging the team and resources you have available to make more time? Be strategic and thoughtful about the time you have. The end result should be a list that is connected to the organization's vision and the vision you maintain for your partnerships. And, when you quickly realize that many of your hours are spent on things that don't matter, don't be discouraged. You can make a change within the next 72 hours. If you don't adjust within the next three days, the chances of you making a lasting change decrease dramatically, so don't wait. Start right now!

Listening To and Filtering Input

People love to give input. Sometimes it can be very helpful and at other times it should be left alone. Be prepared for comments and input from every corner when you start to verbalize and share you vision. Whether that is your personal vision or the vision for the organization, there will be plenty of comments. When sharing the organization's vision, you are hoping to inspire others to get on board and help make it a reality. You will find a select group that does just that and are ready, willing, and able to participate and help. And there will be another group that will stand back and watch your success or failure from a comfortable distance.

Both groups will offer their opinions and you should be sure to listen to each perspective. Work to understand their points and where they are coming from. While you should listen to all opinions, be sure you filter the comments you hear and keep moving forward.

Do not easily get swayed from the task at hand. I have met many brilliant people that have a great idea and vision only to end up jumping onto the next project too quickly. Or they are constantly trying to merge these new comments and ideas with the original vision and it becomes something that is unrecognizable, rarely motivating, and not actionable. Stay the course and make sure you have sufficiently accomplished your task at hand. This does not mean you don't consider their comments and input or that you allow other opportunities to pass you by. You can find a way to do both if something compelling is presented. But remember, one common trait among really successful entrepreneurs is a sense of focus. They are typically so passionate about that one idea and it is all-consuming. Find a balance that works for you and your organization.

Once you clearly communicate the vision, it will be important to get people engaged. How can they support the effort? What are the innovations that will change the landscape? There are several ways to drive innovation. Read stories about companies like 3M, Apple, Google, and others. Understanding how these companies have integrated innovation and creativity into their business models can be very helpful. For your group or organization, be sure to provide a framework or boundaries for innovation. It is unlikely that your vision will become a reality by doing everything exactly the same as you are doing it today. Innovation will be necessary to achieve your vision. Sometimes it comes not from a place of big sky thinking but from a demand on the team to do more with less. This can mean restrictions on budgets or staffing. Amazing innovations and breakthroughs occur when people are set the task of making changes and saving money. It doesn't matter if you are asking people to do more or do less, the key is being able to explain how that action relates to the larger vision and helps the organization move forward.

The vision created by Nike and the Foundation during the LIVESTRONG wristband campaign encouraged participation. In the case of the wristband, other groups and individuals immediately wanted to get involved. The vision was something that allowed everyone to see a better future within the cancer community with their involvement. Other cancer charities began picturing a world where millions of people visibly showed their commitment to the cause. It stirred people's imaginations.

Are You a Visionary?

The point at which someone is deemed a visionary is subjective. That moment at the golf tournament when I first heard the thoughts surrounding the color yellow, Lance, and the cancer community, I knew I was witnessing a visionary at work. But, it wasn't until a couple of months later, when the wristband idea was presented, that I really knew the visionary skills that our Nike champion was leveraging to impact our cause.

Visionaries are not just born. Being a visionary is a learned skill and is not impossible for anyone. Visionaries are connectors of ideas, people, places, and emotions. Visionaries are expert question askers. They ask the right questions—smart questions. While most people were thinking about the next major donor dinner or how to leverage Lance's upcoming Tour competition, our Nike champion was searching for something bigger. I have heard the recommendations to "close your door and think—it's what you get paid for" or "set time aside to dream." But the greatest visions have come from people that spend the maximum amount of time in the communities they hope to improve; engaging with the people that might influence their thoughts and being open to the possibility of a new concept that might just be "the one."

Take a look at how you are spending your time. Be sure you are making a conscious effort to be in the right places and spending time with people who will spark your imagination or further your understanding of the issues. Think about the questions you should ask. When you have a flash of brilliance, and you will, know what to do with it and think about taking those ideas and making them a reality.

Another recommendation is to think multiple years past your current vision. You have painted a picture of the world you envision. You have stories that help engage people in that vision. They are becoming motivated to take action. You have made sure there are no roadblocks in the way of your group's success including giving people the tools to filter out opportunities that don't fit. Just when you thought your work was finished and you could relax, you should be thinking about how to spend the next one, five, or 20 years working toward that vision or understanding how the vision will evolve. And beyond that, spend time thinking about what the organization would look like 10 years after that vision has become a reality. This might seem like an exercise in futility because there would be so many variables, but it is helpful to spend the time considering the possibilities. This line of thought might also cause you to refine your current vision. It will certainly keep you one step ahead of the competition.

*   *   *

I relate the early years at the Foundation to being back in school. It was a time of struggling with the question, "What are you going to be when you grow up?" Our team could see the cancer landscape and we knew we wanted to do something different, but what? We saw other models that were being used to move other causes forward. But we weren't quite sure if or how we should apply those models to our organization. Through careful consideration and much deliberation, the Foundation landed on a vision to serve cancer survivors—to empower them.

"Keep your dreams alive. Understand to achieve anything requires faith and belief in yourself, vision, hard work, determination, and dedication. Remember all things are possible for those who believe."
—Gail Devers

Today, LIVESTRONG is strong, resourceful, flexible, impactful, practical, and more. When asked if he was surprised about the sale of more than 70 million wristbands, our Nike champion responded, "There are six billion people on the planet and every one of them has been touched by cancer. We're just getting started." The staff at the Foundation strove to be the one place

every cancer survivor would call at the point of diagnosis. We used to think about the possibility of that
being the case when we were working in 2001. It was
hard to imagine being the one place every cancer
survivor would call at the point of diagnosis. That was
when we were a staff of five and had one program
person on the team. It was quite an ambitious vision.
What's yours?

Epilogue

Living the Dream

After the wristband campaign, the Lance Armstrong Foundation (Foundation) continued to experience amazing success. In 2004, the Foundation launched LIVESTRONG SurvivorCare and began publishing a 1–800 number for people to call at the point of diagnosis and the concept of a formalized patient navigation was born within the organization. That same year, the Foundation released the National Action Plan for Cancer Survivorship with the Centers for Disease Control and Prevention (CDC) and hosted the inaugural Community Program Conference, Building a Community of

Hope. And supporters of our cause went to Washington D.C. for our inaugural LIVESTRONG Day.

2004 was also the year that my husband and I became first-time parents and welcomed our son Carter Edward into the world. I remember being one week away from my due date at the time of the Austin Gala and enjoyed being able to share in that initial pilot launch of the wristband with our closest friends and supporters.

By 2005, the Foundation had sold more than 55 million wristbands. The ever-expanding group of grassroots fundraisers had raised more than $7 million for the Foundation. The organization began activating the CDC National Action Plan for Cancer Survivorship. The LIVESTRONG Young Adult Alliance was launched and the Foundation quickly rallied to the aid of victims of Hurricane Katrina by awarding $500,000 in assistance to the cancer community impacted by the natural disaster. The entire world celebrated with Lance as he won his record-breaking seventh Tour de France.

2006 was a year of change and growth for the Foundation and for my family. Two years after the launch of the wristband, the message had spread worldwide and the Foundation responded by hosting the first-ever LIVESTRONG Summit. In June of that year, my husband and I celebrated the birth of our second son, Evan Michael. And just before I left the organization in the fall of 2006, the Foundation launched the LIVESTRONG Challenge. What started as the Ride for the Roses had become a weekend filled with events including runs, walks, and rides in multiple cities across the nation.

In 2007, locally in Austin, the LIVESTRONG Survivorship clinic opened at the Dell Children's Medical Center of Central Texas and set a model for future programming and in-facility resources. And in just a few short years, the concept of survivorship and quality of life after cancer, which were not widely discussed in 2000, had become a common phrase used by healthcare professionals, patients, loved ones, the cancer community, and the general public.

Although I was no longer at the Foundation, I continued to be involved in the cancer community. I joined the Board of Directors for Fertile Hope, a fertility resource for cancer survivors, and served as the Development Chairperson.

Throughout the years, Lance has continued to fight for the cancer community. Nike also continued their involvement with the launch of the LIVESTRONG product line, which included everything from hats to shoes benefiting the Foundation. In 2009, the LIVESTRONG Global Cancer Campaign launched and traveled around the world, from Australia to Mexico to Italy throughout the year. LIVESTRONG hosted the 2009 LIVESTRONG Global Cancer Summit, which brought together more than 500 world leaders, corporations, non-governmental organizations, and advocates. While LIVESTRONG was expanding internationally, I was opening the doors to Armbruster Consulting in Austin, Texas. My vision was to help others seeking to do good by sharing the knowledge and experiences I had gained over the course of my career including the six amazing years at the Lance Armstrong Foundation. This was also the year that Fertile Hope was acquired by the Foundation and my board membership transitioned to a position on the Fertility Advisory Committee. It was wonderful to work as the Board liaison between the Lance Armstrong Foundation and Fertile Hope during the process and to experience first-hand how the resources raised from the wristband and other development efforts would allow the programs of Fertile Hope to expand exponentially. My colleague and friend, Bianca Bellavia also transitioned to her new role as the Director of Special Programming at Seton Foundations, lending them her communication and marketing expertise.

2011 has been extremely active for those team members that were a part of the wristband campaign. Lance Armstrong officially returned to fighting cancer full time and spending time with his growing family. After working as a strategic consultant for various companies and nonprofit organizations, Randall Macon developed My Entrepreneurial Journey where he now serves as CEO. Tiffany Galligan also started her own consulting firm called Too Good Strategy.

Many of the early board members and advisors all continue to be deeply involved in the Foundation and passionate about helping it succeed and grow. My mother and father are happily retired and love to reminisce about their merchandise committee days at the Foundation. Thankfully, my mom, who was my initial motivation to join the Foundation in 2000, just celebrated her thirteenth year of being cancer free. There are countless others including the entire development team, all of our volunteers, every rider, walker, and runner, sponsors, and the cancer survivors we represented who helped make this entire journey possible and so much fun.

Looking back, I am eternally grateful for the opportunity I had to work in a place where so much good was possible. The experiences I shared, the mentorship, and sense of purpose were beyond compare. I hold each relationship that started from the Foundation close to my heart. I love running into friends, vendors, riders, or volunteers either around town or while working on new projects. We always smile and share a huge hug and inevitably begin telling stories from "the old days." As a member of the Fertility Advisory Committee at the Foundation, I have the opportunity to run into Lance and Doug occasionally and continue to admire their focus and sense of vision.

Lance always talks about the obligation of the cured which was a term his doctor, Dr. Craig Nichols, shared with him after he had completed all of his treatments. Lance took that call to action seriously and he hasn't stopped fighting for cancer survivors since. I was blessed to be a part of this amazing campaign and such a wonderful organization. Being a part of the Foundation was simply life changing. Having been given that opportunity to be a part of something so monumental, I feel an obligation to share the experience in the hopes that others can learn from it, expand on the lessons learned, and do great things for their own causes. As I mentioned, my hope is that my professional legacy is not the LIVESTRONG wristband campaign itself but rather the millions of other partnerships, dollars raised, and lives impacted by the inspiration it provides for the leaders in our communities.

Exercises and Notes

1. What three books will you read in the next six months on this topic?
2. Write down the names of three people you will discuss this book with. Hopefully you will share the parts you enjoyed, pieces you plan to put into action, and those concepts that you feel could be expanded on or revised. Just have the conversation!
3. Write your story. There is power in being able to convey your own personal story. If corporate relations are largely based on your personal relationships, how do you communicate about yourself? What will people find interesting? Don't just give a timeline of your life but think of this as a short highlight reel—what images would flash on the screen?

4. Write the story for your organization. Same rules apply as your personal story. Maybe you have an interesting founder or maybe the organization experienced significant growth at some point in its evolution. Again, think about the highlight reel and practice saying what you have written. See what people key into and work to refine this and make it more exciting each time you say it.

5. Make a list of your most successful partnerships. Now think about why they work and how those elements can be transferred or built into future relationships.

6. Make a list of the partnerships that did not renew or prospects that ended up not closing and making an impact for your organization. Why did it not work out? What lessons did you learn from those experiences? Have you ensured that they won't happen again by making revisions in the process?

7. Work to expand your relationships and your network.

   a. Write the names of three people in the office you will spend time with this month.

   b. Write the names of three people externally that you will spend time with this month.

   c. Make a list of three people you want to talk to personally this year. These should feel like a stretch and require you to make connections to get introduced.

8. How are you making the partnering process fun for everyone? Cause-marketing relationships should be fun! You are doing work that will make the world a better place—that is not meant

to be boring or stressful. Do people look forward to your calls and meetings? What can you do to make them more exciting?

9. Make an inventory of your relationships and separate them into three groups: A, B, and C. A's are those individuals that you should be talking to on a regular basis. B's are people that you talk to once a month. C's are people you communicate with quarterly. All three groups should receive some type of scheduled communication from you, either through simple emails or handwritten notes, blog posts, forwarding interesting articles, or e-newsletters.

10. Create a clear vision for where you want to go. Define success for you and for the organization. Does it mean impressions and acknowledgement of the brand or does it mean you are in every retail outlet in a certain region? You cannot work toward something if you don't know what it looks like. After you have created this vision, share it. Talk to your team, share it with your partners, your constituents, everyone. Each person can play a part in making that vision a reality.

Partnership Self-Test

Rate the following list 1 through 5, where,

1 = Poor
2 = Average
3 = Good
4 = Very Good
5 = Awesome

1. I know that relationships are my number-one priority.
2. People genuinely enjoy me.
3. I feel comfortable meeting new people.
4. I live my life for others and help people frequently with no direct or immediate gain.
5. I generate useful content and distribute it effectively.
6. I speak at industry events.
7. Powerful people in my industry know me by name.
8. People reach out to me when they are looking to connect or need to expand their networks.
9. I know my story and can tell it at any time, at any place, and to anyone.
10. I know the story of my organization and it is compelling.
11. I have fun and enjoy my work and people can see that when we interact.
12. I am constantly looking for new partner ideas and activation concepts.
13. I know the metrics that matter most, and I monitor and analyze them regularly.
14. I know the metrics that matter most to my partners, and I am monitoring them regularly.
15. I have a clear vision for where I am headed and where my organization is headed.

Scoring the Test

75: Wonderful! Put down the book and get moving! You are ready and nothing can stop you! PS—send out some thank you notes. You didn't get a 75 without surrounding yourself with great people.

60–74: You are doing great and just need a few more tools to help you achieve your goals. Keep working hard and don't lose momentum. Put yourself out in the public more and dedicate the time to reaching out both individually and to groups. The exposure will force you to get better across the board.

45–59: Being just good enough won't solve the world's problems. This is a great time to take inventory and see how you can get those scores up. Find people that you think would have a score of more than 60 and see how they might be able to help you. You will get out of this effort as much or as little as you put in. Make it a priority and strive for excellence in every encounter.

15–44: On the bright side, you have nowhere to go but up! Prioritize the items you think you can handle quickly so you can gain some confidence early on in the process. Work on your story or find three people you can help this week. Then make your way through the remainder of the checklist. It will take time but your cause, your organization, and you need this if you are to be successful and really create a lasting impact. Commit to these changes today.

Conversation Starters for Partnerships and Various Interactions

Do's

1. Have you heard about...?
2. What advice can you share about...?

3. What has your experience been with...?
4. What are you passionate about?
5. What was the most recent book you read?
6. What can I do to help you?
7. Tell me about yourself.
8. How do you spend your free time?

Don'ts

1. Don't start by asking what someone does for a living.
2. Don't talk about yourself first or say a ton of "me/I" phrases during the conversation.
3. Don't pitch the partnership before you know anything about them.
4. Don't look around for someone more important while someone is already taking the time to talk to you.
5. Don't walk away without exchanging cards or contact information.
6. Don't forget to send thank you notes.
7. Don't forget to connect using social media (LinkedIn, Facebook, Twitter, etc.).
8. Don't undervalue what you have to offer others.
9. Don't try to be anyone else—be authentic. People can tell when you're not.

Getting Ready for Success!

The following are some of the questions I ask clients when they are seeking to develop a strong cause-marketing and corporate-relations program. Working together we usually uncover the things that are working well and those areas that need improvement. These questions can help you think about the process and whether or not you have the resources to deploy a successful corporate partnership. This will get the conversations started and help you begin to lay out a path toward your vision.

1. How would you respond if Nike called you today and offered to work with you to create a cause-marketing campaign? What would you say? What would you send them? Who would be involved? Does everyone know their part and would they be ready?

2. What makes you special? What assets do you have to leverage?

   HINT: Don't just say that your walk is an asset. There are lots of walks. Work on filling in the blanks: Our walk is special because _____. Example: Our walk is special because it is the largest gathering of people affected by or passionate about cancer in the country.

3. What are your key messages by audience and the proof points for each statement? Have you prepared efficiently internally before you present externally?

4. How do you make your offering digestible and desirable?

   RED FLAG: If you find yourself going into every presentation with a presentation that includes every conceivable partner-engagement strategy and you leave the filtering and customization to the prospect you have failed to do your job. You must get to know them and help create a path of engagement for them to your organization. Help them help you.

5. Do you have a prospect list? How do you currently filter and prioritize the list? Do you spend more time reacting to incoming requests or proactively approaching the partners you feel make the most sense for your organization and your goals?

6. After you have closed the deal with Nike and you are determining your campaign strategy, how do you activate this new relationship? What account-management structure do you have in place? Are you prepared to connect with the partner at various points (marketing, foundation, and sales)? Do you have a plan in place to steward the new partner from day one and how are you introducing and networking them within your connections?

7. What is your renewal process to ensure high retention rates? Do you have a timeline and have you set calendar reminders to trigger the conversations?

8. How will you engage the partner so they can learn more about your organization and potentially see additional opportunities to expand the relationship? What touch points do you currently have on the calendar?

9. How do you plan to communicate and incorporate other members of your organization (i.e., chapters)? Is an incentive plan offered to help generate partner leads? Do you have regular communication methods that can be utilized to

promote partnerships and monitor benefits delivery?

10. How will you evaluate existing relationships? What is the process for determining moving forward or parting ways?

11. How quickly could you do all of the things mentioned in this list?

Creating Experiences that Become Meaningful Moments

Here is a list of some of my most memorable moments during the LIVESTRONG campaign. When you are reading this list, perhaps you can get a few ideas for your own work regarding what could make your campaign and its overall experience last.

Peloton Project dinner at Lance's house with live music by Lyle Lovett

In the early days of the Ride for the Roses Weekend, we worked hard to create once-in-a-lifetime memories for those riders who worked tirelessly all year to raise funds for the Lance Armstrong Foundation. Lance and Lyle had become friends and he was able to make the request that Lyle perform for our top 200 fundraisers. Here we were, surrounded by a passionate and motivated group of people, just relaxing with Lance and his talented musician friends celebrating life and all that had been accomplished that year. Be sure to create once-in-a-lifetime moments for your staff and your greatest supporters.

Every Ride for the Roses event—start to finish

Every event producer finds him or herself focused on the tasks at hand when events are getting close. Be sure to stop and take a look around and realize all the excitement and happiness that has been created. This also applies to your event participants. Be sure that in between the hustle of activities, they are given a moment to really enjoy the event and go home with stories that will motivate and inspire others.

Working with the development team

There were so many amazing people that worked as part of the development team. Each one left a mark on our campaigns and initiatives. Enjoy those you are working with and make sure you are ready to make changes that seem hard but are necessary in order to create a winning team. I was surrounded by people that forced me to be better every day, and that made me laugh. Don't forget to laugh.

Working late nights in the tiny yellow house at 12th and Lamar and sharing my desk with the first Foundation intern

You cannot get into this line of work and be afraid of long hours and late nights. I have wonderful memories of my husband, Brandon, working with me stuffing invitations, making copies, or sorting T-shirts. It was a team effort and I was thinking about the cause and our mission 24/7. I did not spend much time thinking about the high-rise offices or administrative staffs that some of my peers were enjoying in other professional paths.

When I started, I realized I needed help. I wasn't afraid to ask for it, whether that meant asking my family or interns. Having been an intern all through college, I knew that they could be a valuable resource but we didn't have the space. So, I made space. I cleared off the other side of my desk and we went to work. Be sure to leverage interns and also never pass up an opportunity to mentor and share your knowledge with others.

Toasting to a successful New York City Gala

The LIVESTRONG NYC Gala was our first time taking an event of this scale to a city outside of Austin. We realized quickly the need to engage professional event planners that live and work within the community. They were able to help us leverage our relationships and make new ones. They also helped us navigate the event process in NYC, which was markedly different from Austin. Recognize the impact an expert can have and don't assume that your talents and knowledge will transfer everywhere you go.

Accompanying Lance on hospital visits

Whenever we had the opportunity, we would make time to visit hospitals and visit with cancer survivors. Everyone was focused on Lance and his words or movements so it was nice to stand in the background and just watch the smiles and the hugs and the impact his visit would have. Try to find opportunities for your staff or donors to experience these mission moments. Schedule them in with your other fundraising or outreach activities.

Managing the Lance event at Gilda's Club Chicago with LauraJane Hyde

When we traveled to Chicago for a series of events, one of our stops included a conversation with Lance at the Gilda's Club Chicago. In order to prepare for this event, I was able to work with their Executive Director, LauraJane. Her spirit, her sense of team, her knowledge of their programs and those they served was inspiring. She was making a difference in people's lives every day. She and I have continued to stay in touch and I consider her a fantastic friend and peer. We talk occasionally about new projects or updates and I always learn something new when we are together. I encourage you to connect with others outside your organization. It will serve you well no matter where you go or what you end up doing.

Hearing the stories from Foundation supporters about how moments at our events changed their lives.

Thinking back on the countless stories that came from our events and organization exchanges, I think of people like Bob Hammer who received some advice from a fellow Peloton member at our gala and decided to postpone treatment and get a second opinion. Because of that exchange, Bob and his wife now have a beautiful family that would not have been possible without that exchange. While you are busy capturing the data of wristbands sold, participants registered, or average donation, be sure to capture and share the amazing stories of impact.

Sharing the LIVESTRONG message including speaking to the students of Kellogg School of Business at Northwestern University and sharing a stage at the Cause Marketing Forum with Nike

Being given the opportunity to share knowledge with others is a gift and it should not easily be overlooked.

Working with Jeff Garvey

Jeff Garvey donated two years of his time to the Lance Armstrong Foundation in addition to being one of our largest supporters. Watching his generosity, ability to lead and motivate, and the way he prioritized his family and enjoyed life were all inspiring. Look at the leaders you are currently working with and make note of the skills and talents you will take away from them.

Attending the Andre Agassi dinner and celebrating my first pregnancy with Lance, Kim Taylor, and Tiffany Craven

Never pass up the opportunity to scope out another event. The Agassi Foundation dinner was amazing, from first-rate talent to a high-dollar live auction. Our team left the event with a million ideas to make our event even better. We also learned about the power of engaging donors on-site and not assuming that they had reached their maximum giving capacity with their table purchase. The year we attended, one of their donors made a matching gift pledge that night inspiring others to give more. He turned their $6 million night into a $12 million evening. Learn from others and take away what you can apply to make your programs and campaigns more effective.

Meeting with the Chicago Events Committee to prepare for our upcoming dinner and private ride

In order to organize the series of events in Chicago, we engaged a small but mighty group of volunteers. Abbie, Greg, Dan, Tim, and Mark worked hard to make sure Lance's visit would be meaningful by developing new relationships and raising significant funds for the Lance Armstrong Foundation. As we prepared, we got to know each other and developed a strong friendship. They were some of the best volunteers I have ever worked with. Appreciating your volunteer relationships cannot be overlooked. These are the relationships that you will remember and have with you for the rest of your life—long past your time with any one organization or event.

Celebrating Lance's Tour de France victory while standing with my mother along the Champs-Élysées

Share these amazing moments with people you love. Use each one as a way to remind yourself of why you are there and how much it means to others.

Celebrating the success of the LIVESTRONG wristbands with the entire staff at Lance's ranch

Lance was always good at celebrating a job well done. It is rewarding to look back on what has been accomplished and can be motivating for the next set of goals and objectives.

The moment at the Golf Tournament Welcome Dinner that Scott MacEachern asked me about the meaning of the color yellow

Every conversation matters. Do not be so busy that you are rushing from person to person and not giving anyone your undivided attention. You never know which conversation could be "the one."

Watching my mom make the sign of the cross on my son's forehead during his baptism and seeing her bright yellow LIVESTRONG wristband

Make it personal. You are working to make the world a better place. This is amazing and fun work. Enjoy it and embrace the fact that this will never be "just a job." Be thankful for that sense of purpose and opportunity to make an impact on people—both professionally and personally.

Resources

Recommended Reading[*]

The Cathedral Within by Bill Shore
Little Black Book of Connections by Jeffrey Gitomer
Referral of a Lifetime by Tim Templeton
Living a Life that Matters by Harold Kushner (not directly applicable but my favorite so it makes the list!)
Season of Life by Jeffrey Marx
It's Not About the Bike by Lance Armstrong
Elegant Solutions by Matthew E. May

[*]Connect via LinkedIn for reading recommendation updates.

Writing Your Story

Before you write your personal story, read Scott Dinsmore's blog post about how to tell a compelling personal story. Blog: Live Your Legend, www. liveyourlegend.com.

Blog Tool

Use Google Reader to keep all of your blogs organized and to help manage the volume of information.

Staying Up to Date and Relevant

Sign up for Google Alerts for every prospect or partner. Be sure to forward them relevant and timely information.

Events to Attend

Cause Marketing Forum
Run Walk Ride
IEG Sponsorship Forum
TED conferences

Presentation Ideas

Visit TED.com and take a look at the various presentation styles and delivery methods. You will get ideas about how you can package and present your content and lots of inspiration!

Online Survey Tools

Survey Monkey
Poll Everywhere
Zoomerang
Doodle

Connect

Use LinkedIn to promote new opportunities, connect with people after your initial meeting, connect others together, measure your networking progress, and to keep up to date on people and their whereabouts.

Me!

Email me at Rachel@rachelarmbruster.com or call 512–944–3417. Connect at www.linkedin.com/in/rachelkarmbruster and on Twitter @rarmbruster.

About the Author

Rachel Armbruster is President of Armbruster Consulting and is an executive nonprofit strategist specializing in fundraising. She lives in Austin, Texas, and has more than 15 years experience in marketing, nonprofit management, and fundraising.

As an executive nonprofit strategist, Rachel is focused on solving revenue, structure, and opportunity challenges in order to maximize the return on investment for charities and their partners. Rachel is dedicated to the success and growth of organizations and is passionate about making positive changes in society. Her client list is a reflection of her philanthropic objectives.

Rachel's extensive background in nonprofit strategies comes from years of dedication to the field, including her role as Vice President of Business Development for Event 360, Inc. where she launched the Autism Society and Pump It Up cause-marketing campaigns and served as a member of the consulting team for multiple nonprofit engagements. Clients often comment about Rachel's breadth of experience and ideas which are highlighted when coming up with out-of-the-box thinking, creative approaches to fundraising, interesting concepts, or new ways to innovate existing programs.

While she was the Director of Development at the Lance Armstrong Foundation (Foundation), Rachel was responsible for creating new fundraising programs, evaluating proposals, and planning for future Foundation revenue. When she started with the organization in 2000, Rachel was one of three employees and was responsible for growing the Ride for the Roses event. From 2000 to 2006, the Foundation grew from an organization with $1 million in annual revenue to a global cancer charity raising more than $40 million a year. One of her many successes at the Foundation was managing the Nike relationship for six years and playing an instrumental role in the launch and management of the LIVESTRONG wristband campaign.

Prior to the Lance Armstrong Foundation, Rachel worked in advertising for SicolaMartin Advertising managing event marketing and on-site branding for one of the agency's strategic technology accounts. While residing in El Paso, Rachel served as the Director of Marketing for the Sun Bowl Association.

Rachel has made it her life's work to assist nonprofit organizations with their fundraising and outreach programs by making them more efficient and effective.

Rachel has been invited to speak at many special training and development conferences, such as the Run Walk Ride Conference, annual IEG Sponsorship Conference, and Kellogg School of Business Marketing Conference. She currently serves on the Fertility Advisory Committee at the Lance Armstrong Foundation. Rachel is a graduate of Purdue University with her Bachelor of Arts degree in Communications and her Masters in Business Administration from St. Edward's University. Rachel lives in Austin with her husband Brandon and is the proud mother of two fantastic boys (Carter, age 7, and Evan, age 5).

Index